THE MODERN DAIRY

NOURISHING RECIPES USING MILK, YOGURT, CHEESE AND CREAM

Discover the science behind this nutritional powerhouse

ANNIE BELL

PHOTOGRAPHY BY CON POULOS

KYLE BOOKS

To
Elizabeth Bell

First published in Great Britain in 2017 by
Kyle Books, an imprint of Kyle Cathie Ltd
192–198 Vauxhall Bridge Road
London SW1V 1DX
general.enquiries@kylebooks.com
www.kylebooks.co.uk

10 9 8 7 6 5 4 3 2 1

ISBN 978 0 85783 358 7

Project Editors: Kyle Cathie and Claire Rogers
Copy Editor: Stephanie Evans
Designer: Erika Oliveira
Design Porduction Assistant: Hollis Yungbliut
Photographer: Con Poulos
Food and Prop Stylist: Susie Theodorou
Recipe Analysis: Alina Tierney
Production: Nic Jones, Gemma John and Lisa Pinnell

A Cataloguing in Publication record for this title is available from the British Library.

Colour reproduction by ALTA London
Printed and bound in China by 1010 International Printing Ltd.

contents

4   Preface

8   **INTRODUCTION**
Milk
Butter
Cheese
Cream
Yogurt
Lactose Intolerance

40   **HOMEMADE**

56   **BOWL OF SOUP**

72   **SOMETHING LIGHT: DIPS, EATS & MELTS**

102   **GRAINS & PASTA**

116   **A NEW LOOK AT SAUCES: ROASTS, GRILLS & STEWS**

134   **VEGGIES**

154   **FRESH & LUXURIOUS SALADS**

170   **CREAMY FINISHES: ICES, CREAM & COMFORTS**

190   Index

192   Acknowledgements

THE TERROIR OF MILK

My passion for dairy finds its roots in a journey I made some twenty years ago. I had been commissioned by *YOU Magazine* to go to Normandy to interview the chef Jean-Christophe Novelli who had recently converted an old watermill into a restaurant. Coincidentally my neighbour, producer/director Max Jourdan, had been booked as the accompanying photographer.

So one morning we squeezed ourselves into his small car along with all the camera cases and tripods and set off for the Cotentin Peninsula, the finger of land that protrudes into the Channel with the port of Cherbourg at its tip. Aside from plenty of lively conversation that saw our journey speed by, my abiding memory is of stepping off the kerb of a dusty West London pavement into the car, and out again onto the soft tread of long grasses on arrival. I had never encountered grass that luscious, every blade having the semblance of a cartoon image, long and straight with neatly tapered ends. It looked as though it had been groomed with a wire brush. And the scent that accompanied it was overwhelmingly heady and sweet.

The Cotentin is something like being on an island. Its eastern shores are fringed with the landing beaches that lead round to the Côte Fleurie, beloved by the Impressionists, while those on the west coast look out towards the (English) Channel Islands and the (French) Iles Chausey. A part of the Cotentin is reclaimed marshes, while another part comprises gently undulating valleys with rivers at their base, salt marshes and estuaries, and ancient heaths. And the weather is wild and unpredictable, squalling in and over the land, misting the pasture with rain.

If you fast forward to today, I have lost count of the number of times I have made that journey to our farmhouse there, a seventeen-century *corps de ferme* that once belonged to the cousin of English diarist John Evelyn, author of the celebrated book *Acetaria*. It lies deep within the dairy country of the *bocage,* a mishmash of medieval fields traced by coppiced hedgerows that look like a patchwork quilt in disarray on an unmade bed. Some of this pasture is unimproved grassland that goes back hundreds and hundreds of years, and has never been ploughed. Unlike farmland further east towards Caen, where it is flat, there has been a move to preserve this arrangement. The result is a continuing tradition of small dairy farms that produce the wonderful butters, *crème crue* (raw unpasteurised cream), fromage frais and cheeses to be found in the local markets.

So those first few steps on the soft Norman turf on arrival continue to enchant me as much now as they did then. They signal the start of feasting on Camembert, Livarot and Pont-l'Évêque, the pungent and creamy cornerstone cheeses of Normandy. These are the cow's milk cheeses born of the milk from the herds that graze freely on those lush, scented grasses, and the quality of their diet translates naturally into these products.

The Modern Dairy

While I write this preface, it is teatime as Jean Legraverand, a third-generation dairy farmer, cordons off the route from the field, where seventy-five Norman cows are grazing in the late afternoon sun of August, to the dairy. With their distinctive dappled chestnut markings and *lunettes* – the two patches over their eyes – I find it hard to take my eyes off them, one of nature's great works of art. Together with the iconic Jersey breed of dairy cattle (pictured), they promise exceptionally rich milk high in butter fat.

They are scattered over four hectares of pasture, some standing, some lying, together in twos and threes or alone. Like large tardy dogs, they instantly recognise his call as he bids them to come for milking, and they start slowly lumbering towards the gate in a funnel of movement. Their response is both learnt and innate: they know the routine, and they also know there is food at the other end and relief for their swollen udders. They form themselves into an orderly line, two by two, as they amble down the narrow lane of dried mud towards the barn.

Jean's operation is as close to free-range as a cow could hope for, and after the evening milking and feeding in the barn, they are at liberty to roam back to the field for the evening. Come the morning, they will have made their own way back to the milking parlour.

Today's reprieve of dairy that allows us to welcome it back into our lives is life-affirming. For many years dairy has proved an easy public health target for initiatives seeking to reduce our intake of saturated fat. But the more studies carried out, the more science advances and the more we learn. The fat component of milk is made up of four hundred different fatty acids with a wide variety of effects, many of which are beneficial to our health. Fat, and in particular saturated fat, is no longer to be feared, respected perhaps, but also relished. And the way it is produced has everything to do with good nutrition.

All too often we find quality and health pulling in different directions, where one is at the expense of the other. So it is both rare, and special, that dairy offers us the best and the healthiest in a single package. The key is that we look to grass-fed cattle and artisanal production instead of grain-fed stock and industrial products that have altered the make-up of dairy over the past sixty years. We nearly all have access to organic milk, and regional traditions by way of fine butters and cheeses, creams and yogurts. The renaissance of this kind of small-scale dairy farming is one that we should cling onto and celebrate. I hope with this book to combine nutrition and how to eat dairy for good health with a love of food and cooking, to bring a little in the way of harmony to this remarkable foodstuff.

THE MAGIC OF DAIRY

The closer you peer through the magnifying glass at milk, the more extraordinary it becomes. We bandy around the expression 'superfood', crowning new ingredients on a monthly basis for their nutrient-rich profile, and yet I cannot think of a single one that comes anywhere close to matching milk. And it's not just with awe at its nutrient content, the range of produce made using this humble liquid is breath-taking, from the yogurts and fromage frais, to the different creams, butters and cheeses. As well as being widely available, most dairy products are affordable, in particular by comparison to sources of protein such as meat or fish. So here you have a complete food, that also offers infinite variety and scope for enjoyment – from the simple pleasure of a sliver of cheese with a select pickle, to the many different ways of including it in both sweet and savoury dishes.

For over forty years, the official guidance for losing weight and staying healthy has revolved around reducing fat and calories, and yet obesity has continued to rise unabated. Over that same time period we have given dairy a wide berth, fearful of what it might do to our cholesterol levels and waistlines. And that is not withstanding the fashionable exclusion of dairy, an irrational avoidance that deprives us of so much benefit – and pleasure – based on the mistaken belief that it is bad for us. Unless you suffer from a specific medical condition linking dairy to your symptoms, there is no evidence to suggest it is in any way detrimental to health; in fact, the opposite is true.

I hope in the course of this book to address any fears or uncertainty with recipes geared towards harnessing dairy's goodness, while treating with caution its wider excess by way of saturated fat and salt. And also to persuade the lactose intolerant to return to the fold by explaining which dairy foods to choose (recipes marked with **LF**).

So this book is no more about rivers of cream on everything than it is about joyless low fat. The recipes take as their foundation rigorous scientific guidelines and evidence in support of consuming the optimum types and amounts of dairy, showing how we can derive all the goodness it has to offer without the pitfalls.

Instead of mash that comes laced with heart-stopping amounts of butter, a sliver added to a potato purée that is otherwise reliant on olive oil will still give you the desired creamy depth and finish without the gratuitous fat or calories. And instead of cooking with a lot of cream, there are sauces that play on half and half: a little crème fraîche or soured cream combined with a low-fat Greek yogurt, or quark, which is virtually fat-free. High-fat cheeses also need treating with some caution, not least for their salt content. Again, by including just enough to get the full benefit of their character, while making olive or rapeseed oil their partners in crime rather than butter, and holding on any additional salt, it ensures that the dish still has a healthy profile.

So it is, if you like, to do with a subtle reshaping. And hopefully the end result will be a fridge and larder stocked with a rich array of dairy produce that will become a mainstay for the way you eat, in the same way as fruit and veg, or pulses and grains.

BUILDING BLOCKS

Before we can work out the best way of including dairy in our diets, we need to take a quick look at the basics – our dietary requirements. Nutrients divide into the three big hitters – carbohydrate, fat and protein – which are the macronutrients that we consume in quantity and from which we derive our energy, and the micronutrients – minerals, vitamins and trace elements – which, in minute quantities, support a vast array of functions within the body that contribute to our well-being and prevent disease.

In a perfect world, there is a very specific optimum prescription of macronutrients given as a percentage of energy intake. That is, we are supposed to derive 50% of our energy needs from carbohydrates. However, no more than 5% of that should come from free sugars, the perceived baddies contained in fizzy drinks and table sugar, which also includes fruit juices and honey. Total fat is not meant to exceed 35% of our energy, and no more than 11% of that should be saturated. Fat is the wild card in dairy products, which can contain anything from 0% to 80% – something akin to the difference between water and brandy in terms of alcohol – hence the need to redefine the best way to enjoy it. Protein is the good friend that parleys between these two players, and in dairy it can account for almost all of the product or very little, meaning it is something that can be used to our advantage.

Most foods contain all three macronutrients, albeit in different proportions, and it is very simple: if a food is high in carbohydrates, then it will be low in fat and protein; if it is high in fat, then it will be low in protein and carbohydrate; and for protein, ditto. So together these nutrients make up a pie chart:

IDEAL

carbohydrate

fat

protein

While most ingredients tend to have a fairly static profile (meat and fish will be high in protein, and fruit high in carbohydrate), dairy is unique in the way that the proportion of the macronutrients can vary markedly between different dairy products. For example, 100g Parmesan contains about 30g fat, 36g protein and 1g carbohydrate, whereas quark contains less than 1g of fat, 14g protein and 4g carbohydrate for the same amount. This is the key to dairy's potential health benefits, as it is uniquely flexible. It can be whatever you want it to be. No other food group can match dairy in that sense.

EAT FAT TO GET THIN?

The quality of a macronutrient is as important as the amount you are consuming. When a diet recommends reducing fat or carbohydrate or protein, what you replace it with is just as relevant to health. Opting for a 'low-fat' strawberry yogurt instead of a full-fat natural yogurt is a step backwards not forwards; the 'low-fat' strawberry version has replaced the butterfat (and its precious micronutrients) with free sugars, which have no nutritional value. They are empty calories, if you like; energy without goodness. This is another reason why low-fat diets have fallen out of favour and diets higher in fat are making a comeback. Dairy fat is nothing to be afraid of or to avoid: it is a high-quality foodstuff, providing we eat it in a way that is discerning.

But certainly there is a growing body of evidence that calls into question the advice to reduce your fat intake either to lose weight or in the interests of reducing chronic disease. As it stands, the official recommendations for fat and saturated fat consumption are generous: the issue with fat is excess not moderation, and the good news is that we can eat a wide variety of dairy produce in a way that is pleasurable without having to compromise within those guidelines. And that is what this book is all about, relishing dairy at the same time as deriving the nutritional benefits it has to offer.

3 A DAY

Nutrition has at its heart an all-consuming aim: the prevention of chronic disease. It is sometimes easy to forget this comparative modesty when it is drowned out by the daily tsunami of wild claims for how chia seeds will render your body beach-ready, and kale in combination with seaweed will turn back the clock by ten years. If that happens too, well that's great, but the more down-to-earth intention is to reduce the risk of those feared spectres of our modern lifestyle: obesity and its companions diabetes and cardiovascular disease, certain cancers and osteoporosis. Perhaps not so modest.

But before we can determine how much dairy we should be eating, we need to look at who we are. There are broad guidelines for energy needs, modified by whether we are male or female, whether we are just out of school or approaching retirement, whether we are gym bunnies or prefer to spend our time off lying in bed watching box sets. And common sense should prevail so that if you are female, diminutive and addicted to watching *Game of Thrones* then you shouldn't try to match the energy intake of your burly male neighbour who is out rowing morning and evening, and chopping logs in between.

These differences aside, adult energy requirements remain stable from the age of nineteen until about sixty, when they start to decline, with the exception of during pregnancy and lactation. An adult man with a low activity level has an estimated average requirement of about 2,500 kcal, while for a woman it is 2,000 kcal.* These figures in turn allow us to calculate how much fat we should be consuming, which is expressed as a percentage of total energy. It means that men should be aiming to consume no more than 31g of saturated fat a day and women 24g a day, the actual recommendation being for 30g and 20g respectively.

The good news is that these are very generous allowances in terms of enjoying dairy produce. The danger zone with dairy is a no-holds-barred river of double cream, that large bowl of ice cream, or an innocent-looking chicken kiev that has half a pack of butter neatly concealed within its breadcrumbed breast. Or it could be that your dairy intake is modest but that a penchant for takeaways, pork belly and sausages pushes your saturated fat over the top. Cereal and baking products also account for as much of our saturated fat intake as dairy, and it is frequently hidden.

I find the most helpful way of including the right amount of dairy in my daily diet is to treat it as I do my 5-a-day fruit and veg, by aiming for 3-a-day of different types. In practice, this changes from one day to the next, so bearing in mind that a portion can include a yogurt of about 150g, a 30g hunk of cheese, or 200ml of milk, this provides a good benchmark to aim for. In short: little and often, and as varied as possible. Variation lies at the heart of good nutrition, a modest amount of everything will always be better than a large amount of just one food.

All the recipes that follow have been devised to keep saturated fat well within the lower limit of a woman's recommended daily intake of 20g, and the majority of dishes contain no more than half that amount, which leaves plenty of scope for whatever else you eat that day.

*Further information can be found at the British Nutrition Foundation: www.nutrition.org.uk

THE DAIRY PARADOX: TRANS FATS

The pursuit of eternal youth affects foodstuffs just as much as people. At one point it looked as though we had perhaps cracked it. Hydrogenated fatty acids or trans fats entered our lives in the 1950s as a means of artificially extending the shelf life of processed foods including many baked goods, snacks and margarine. The chemical process of hydrogenating oils means that they stay solid at room temperature, which inhibits the ability of bacteria, water and so forth to enter the space and spoil the food. So far, so brilliant. But then the bad news started to trickle in, as scientific studies concluded that artificial trans fats can cause profound damage to blood vessels. This evil is not exaggerated: if 2% of total energy comes from artificial trans fatty acids, it raises the risk of coronary heart disease by a whopping 23%. Today reformulation has resulted in a significant reduction in the use of trans fats, but their reputation is soiled and lingers on.

And this is where it becomes intriguing. The only naturally occurring trans fatty acids are found in foods deriving from ruminants – which includes dairy products. For reasons not fully understood, naturally occurring trans fats do not seem to carry the

same risks, but have an inverse protective effect on coronary heart disease. So we have a paradox here of artificial versus natural, with radically opposing effects of either posing a high risk to health or actively protecting it. This enigma is something that we will almost certainly hear more about in future, but for the time being it is good for dairy lovers to know that the trans fats found naturally in dairy products are doing them more good than harm.

GRASS VERSUS GRAIN-FED

Before my elderly neighbours in Normandy retired, their life was a microcosm of a *paysan's* way of life as it might have been before postwar mechanisation, and industrialisation of farming practices took hold. Their days were spent tending a smallholding with a pig, a poultry coop with chicken, guinea fowl and turkey, a small veg plot, and a few cows. Madame Marriette would venture into the field opposite twice a day, carrying her three-legged stool, and milk the cows by hand, before transporting the milk back to the farmhouse in buckets at either end of a yoke slung across her shoulders.

At our farmhouse in Normandy we are surrounded by such smallholders and dairy farmers. They graze their cattle on the rich pasture all year round, save for a brief period over the winter when it is too cold and wet and the grass has stopped growing, when the cows are kept indoors and fed on silage. And the milk, butter and cream to be found in the local market mirrors the season and the pasture. The richest and most fragrant milk is produced around May, when cows have grazed in fields full of wild flowers, buttercups and dandelions. The way in which summer and winter milks differ is a reflection of their complexity and their compound make-up.

Dairy farming and husbandry in industrialised countries have seen drastic changes since the Second World War. In 1940, 99% of cattle in the US were farmed within herds with fewer than 30 milk cows. Today, most of its farms are large-scale operations of high-yield breeds such as Holsteins, or, in the UK, a Holstein-Friesian cross, raised mainly on a high-energy protein diet to maximise output. The herds are kept indoors and fed largely on fodder containing grains, soya and added micronutrients. The aim is for milk that has a consistent nutritional quality throughout the year, and it is very different in profile to that produced by my Norman neighbouring farmer, which is milk that is naturally dictated by the quality of the pasture and the seasons. Those time-honoured artisanal methods of production, where outdoor grazing is the foundation, offer the same benefits wherever dairy is produced in the world.

The most recent scientific research is seeing dairy enjoy something of a reprieve from its reputation of old that saw it linked to obesity. There is robust evidence to suggest that it is inversely associated with weight gain, with no correlation to either diabetes or cardiovascular disease. Given that the many unusual fatty acids contained in dairy fat have been reduced by modern farming practices as well as through the de-creaming of milk, it may be that we are consuming far fewer, when they are biologically active and possibly advantageous to weight control, insulin sensitivity and glucose tolerance.

So there is good reason to believe that it is the quality of dairy fat rather than dairy fat per se that is at fault. Fatty acids contained in dairy fat are biologically active, and the content of these is steered by the feed of the cow, in particular fresh grass, its natural diet. The upshot of the science is that, while we can't travel back in time, as consumers we can use our awareness to benefit nutritionally.

One assured route is organic dairy produce. The standards are likely to differ marginally from one country to another, but within the UK for instance, after weaning, 60% of the dairy herd's diet must consist of organic grass and clover, or conserved forage and roots, only modestly supplemented with cereals or pulses. And the cattle must be allowed to graze on fresh forage throughout the grazing season. This is a far cry from intensively reared cattle that never see a blade of grass and are fed on grains. In many countries, the renaissance of small-scale artisanal farms provides us with another route in. So when you find yourself standing at the chill counter gazing at the display of dairy products that seems to disappear into the distance, the word 'organic' is a good starting point.

MINERALS AND VITAMINS

Calcium

The chalky mineral that we know as calcium accounts for a staggering 99% of bones and teeth. And it is just as well that we have a lot of it, given the physiological function known as calcium homeostasis, which is our making as well as potentially our undoing. It is one of the great marvels of the way the body works. If you have noticed that a doctor never offers you a calcium blood test, this is because, unless there was some underlying malfunction, it would appear normal regardless of how much calcium you obtain from your food. Our bones act as a seemingly limitless calcium bank and they maintain blood calcium levels. If for some reason there is a drop in blood calcium, it will borrow from this bank to recreate the status quo. So, if your diet is deficient in calcium, it is the bones that are robbed, not the blood.

And herein lies the great danger associated with insufficient calcium intake: this process of borrowing can go on for years with no symptoms, and it is only in later life when it becomes apparent that bone integrity has been compromised. When you consider that in the UK 40% of women over the age of 50 will suffer a fragility fracture as a result of osteoporosis (the loss of bone density) at some point of their lives, the contribution of those three portions of dairy a day gains in magnitude. Osteoporosis is aptly known as the silent disease.

The calcium content of milk is dairy's great claim to fame. In fact, no other food comes close. A 200ml glass of milk offers up 240mg of calcium. And for concentrated dairy, this shoots up even higher. Edam cheese, for instance, has 795mg of calcium per 100g. To put this in perspective, the closest contender is half a can of sardines (with bones), which contains about 260mg, while the same quantity of canned salmon has only 47mg, and two spears of broccoli just 34mg. So by eating your 3 a day, you will have pretty much sewn up your dietary requirement for calcium with little further ado. And even better news, calcium is not affected by fat content, so we can eat and enjoy dairy foods in a way that suits our palates.

CALCIUM REQUIREMENTS

525mg per day	Infants under 1yr
350 / 450 / 550 mg per day	Children 1–3 / 4–6 / 7–10yrs
800 / 1,000mg per day	Adolescents 11–18 yrs (girls / boys)
700mg per day	Adults
1,250mg per day	Breastfeeding mothers
1,000mg per day	Adults with osteoporosis
1,200mg per day	Women past menopause
1,200mg per day	Men over 55yrs
1,000 to 1,500mg per day	Adults with coeliac disease
1,000 / 1,200mg per day	Adults with inflammatory bowel disorders (under / over 55yrs)

Our needs for calcium and ability to absorb it change throughout our lifecycle. From birth until around the age of twenty we are actively growing, achieving peak bone mass somewhere between about twenty and thirty years. After this age we gradually lose bone, when resorption exceeds formation. This is why peak bone mass is so crucial, and the marker for future risk of fractures. It also explains why dairy is such a valuable food source for young people. Children in particular may not be able to meet their calcium needs without it.

Multi-vitamins

Dairy produce is incredibly rich in micronutrients, especially vitamins. Whole milk (but not skimmed), is a good source of fat-soluble vitamin A in the form of retinol and carotene, which promote good vision. Dairy also contains fat-soluble vitamin K, essential to blood clotting, and is another vitamin with a role to play in bone formation. It is also a good source of water-soluble B vitamins – B1 (thiamine), B2 (riboflavin), B3 (niacin), B5 (pantothenate), B6 (pyridoxine), B7 (biotin), B12 (cobalamin and related forms) and folate. Among the B vitamins' essential functions, B12 is needed for the production of red blood cells and for nerve function, while B2 is a coenzyme that plays a role in releasing energy. The mineral iodine is needed to make thyroid hormones that contribute to our metabolism. Dairy is also a source of phosphorus and potassium.

Vitamin D

It is sometimes claimed that dairy contains lots of vitamin D, which isn't entirely true, unless it has been fortified, and that is sometimes the case given this micronutrient's essential role in the absorption of calcium. Without vitamin D, the body cannot make use of calcium to grow or maintain healthy bones; it simply passes through the system unabsorbed. So vitamin D merits a slightly closer look, especially since many of us are deficient in it, adolescents in particular, who then run the risk of not reaching peak bone mass.

Most of our vitamin D is synthesised in the skin through the action of sunlight, which contains ultraviolet B (UVB) radiation. The amount of UVB in the solar spectrum is determined by the height of the sun, and this in turn is a function of latitude, the season and time of day. So it is greatest during the summer months, in the UK for instance from March through to September. And it decreases with increasing latitudes and as the days become shorter. One upshot of this is that we go outdoors less and tend to wrap up when it's cold. So during these months we become increasingly reliant on dietary sources. These, however, are few and far between, and derive mainly from animal sources such as egg yolks and oily fish – wild mushrooms too. So easy enough to see why so many of us become deficient in vitamin D during the winter months. Those people with dark skin and the elderly are at even greater risk due to the slow rate at which vitamin D is synthesised through the skin.

It comes as a shock to be reminded of the occasional reappearance of rickets in children in developed countries when it was considered to be a disease of the past. Rickets is a crippling condition caused by a vitamin D deficiency that results in severely bowed legs (it continues to afflict children in China, Mongolia, sub-Saharan Africa, the Middle East and Latin America). In part its reappearance in the West has been put down to the use of sunblock, and that children don't play outside as much as they used to. Even a low sunscreen of SPF8 will reduce vitamin D synthesis, although with up to SPF30 it does still take place if we spend about 10–20 minutes a day in sunlight. But otherwise, exposing your hands, face and arms (without sunscreen) between April and September for 5–10 minutes between 11am and 3pm two to three times a week should be sufficient to ensure that you are getting enough vitamin D if you have pale skin; while those with dark skin and the elderly need to spend longer in the sun.

Note: There is a recommendation in the UK for the population aged 4 years and over, including pregnant and lactating women, of a RNI (Reference Nutrient Intake) of 10µg vitamin D per day throughout the year as a precautionary measure. For children below the age of 4 years, there is a recommended 'safe intake' of vitamin D per day of 8.5–10µg aged 0–1 year (including exclusively breast-fed and partially breast-fed infants from birth) and 10µg aged 1–4 years. In sunnier climes these recommendations may change.

MILK

The calm white of milk belies its sophistication. The dazzling array of regional produce from around the world that results from this liquid is down to an extraordinary union of climate, soil and grass, the animals and the hands that tend them. Dairy is a bedrock of the way that people eat in the West, coursing through the culture of how we eat.

Milk is a perfect, complete foodstuff. It is the means by which all mammals nurture their newborn offspring, and the only food needed to survive during those early days. Within the base of water it contains proteins, fats, carbohydrate or sugar in the form of lactose, salts, vitamins and minerals. Milk is unique; it has never been successfully replicated in an artificial form.

Complete nutrition

While milk contains the full complement of vitamins and minerals, most of these are in trace form only. Calcium is the principal salt, and the micronutrient we most closely associate with dairy. We can also make great use of vitamin A, which contributes to normal vision, the maintenance of our skin, normal iron metabolism and our immune systems, and also carotene, which gives the milk its ivory hue. This is why we hear so much about whole versus skimmed milk, because the latter has this valuable vitamin stripped out. Fat plays the role of messenger, and carries the fat-soluble vitamins and essential fatty acids, as well as contributing about half milk's energy content.

Carbohydrate takes the form of the sugar lactose, while the type of protein that concerns us most is casein, which is separated out from the milk in cheese-making in the form of curds, usually through the action of rennet, an enzyme produced in a calf's stomach.

Pasteurisation

Most milk, aside from a niche market in raw dairy, will have been heat treated (or pasteurised). The idea is to extend its shelf life by going to war against bacteria and killing them off, while inactivating enzymes that would result in unsavoury flavours. The rich nutrient profile of milk is also its potential undoing, making it the perfect environment for any number of harmful microbes to thrive and multiply, the best known being tuberculosis. And it is readily contaminated.

Of the various routes to pasteurisation, they all hark back to their founder, the nineteenth-century scientist Louis Pasteur. First the milk is heated to kill potentially harmful micro-organisms, then rapidly cooled and stored.

Homogenisation

Eric the milkman played a big part in my childhood. Six days a week he could be relied upon to deliver milk to our door in time for breakfast. Depending on whether my mother had set the dial on the milk rack from 1 to 6, and also to gold, silver, green, red or blue tops, he would leave the requisite bottles.

The foil bottle tops were colour-coded to represent their cream content, which ranged from decadently rich to thin and delicate. We were a silver-top family, somewhere in the middle, and I do recall my father hitting the roof at my indulgent teenage habit of opening bottle after bottle to skim off the conical head of cream for my morning cornflakes, leaving the loveless skimmed milk below for his coffee. So, yes, nostalgia plays its part in my finding the uniformity of homogenised milk uncharacterful and bland, and one less potentially bad but delicious habit in the offing.

Homogenisation is the process of filtration that renders milk a uniform colour and consistency. Left to their own devices, fat molecules, being lighter than liquid milk, settle on the surface – hence that head of cream. Such milk is still around, though usually only the richest escapes homogenisation.

The ever-resourceful French invented the procedure of forcing milk at high pressure through a fine nozzle onto a hard surface. This modifies the fat globules to an even size, about a quarter of the original, thus spreading the fats evenly through the milk, which explains its uniformly white appearance, and makes it more convenient to use.

TYPES OF MILK

Different countries will have different varieties of milk depending on their fat content, and in the UK it has for many years been a choice of three, although there is a new milk on the block for those who cannot choose between skimmed and semi-skimmed. The good news is that they have similar micronutrient profiles (especially on the calcium front); the main difference is the retinol and carotene contents, which are fat-dependent (see page 15). So whereas skimmed milk has 1mg and a trace respectively, whole milk has 33mg and 20mg per 100ml.

Skimmed milk has the least fat at 0.5g per 100ml and it has a slightly higher level of calcium than whole milk, but lower levels of fat-soluble vitamins, in particular vitamin A.

Semi-skimmed milk the most widely consumed milk in the UK, has 1.7g fat per 100ml.

Whole milk contains on average 3.9g fat per 100ml.

Channel Islands (Jersey and Guernsey) milk also known as breakfast milk, is the richest milk at 5g fat per 100ml. As it contains more fat than other milks it is also richer in vitamin A.

Organic milk has the same micronutrient profiles but, importantly, it is produced by cows grazed on pasture with no chemical fertilisers, pesticides or agrochemicals. If you can, make organic your default choice.

Sterilised and UHT (Ultra Heat Treated) milk has been processed in a way that extends its shelf life, but neither is preferable to fresh milk, given their unnatural flavour. Sterilised also has a lower nutritional value, in particular vitamins B and C, and both milks lose folate and vitamin B12 due to reactions with oxygen present in the packaging. UHT keeps the longest, but at a cost of acquiring a pervasive cooked flavour.

milk

Unpasteurised (raw) milk is a niche market, one that you might come across at a farmer's market, and it is not unusual across Europe. While it cannot be bought at supermarkets in the UK, it can, however, be found in supermarkets in France.

Other types of milk are not uncommon; goat's and sheep's milks are deliciously creamy, and lactose-free milks are also increasingly available.

Boiling and cooking with milk

When I was a child, and a hot milky drink at night was the norm, so was a small milk saucepan with a glass disc permanently in it that usefully rattled when the milk came to the boil, preventing the drama of it boiling over. Few of us keep such kit to hand, but there are certain guidelines that help when heating milk.

Milk has a tendency to catch on the base of the pan and burn because the casein particles (micelles) and whey proteins sink. A non-stick pan is the best way to side step this, and keep it over a medium heat to avoid overheating the corners or the sides.

Because milk also takes offence at a wide variety of ingredients that can cause it to curdle, cooking with it can be a hit-and-miss process. To be on the safe side, I try to avoid using it as a simmering medium, and prefer to cook ingredients separately and then combine them. This said, if you do, for instance, decide to poach smoked haddock or potatoes in milk, do so over a very gentle heat.

Taste of milk

I never think of milk as having much taste; if anything, it is the sugars that come through, and also the cream content. Unpasteurised milk will have a richer flavour profile than pasteurised in its uncooked state, hense the superior quality of many unpasteurised cheeses, butters and creams. In cooking with it, however, you effectively pasteurise it and are back to square one. Otherwise, while skimmed milk might hit the spot for a cup of tea, there are occasions when a creamy milk is desirable, in a cake, a soup, a white sauce. And breakfast milk is aptly named for the way in which it will transform a bowl of porridge.

Storage

Back in the days when milk was delivered daily by a milk van, it is unlikely that my mother was aware that milk exposed to bright sunlight for several hours can lose up to 70% of its riboflavin, and vitamin C can reduce to virtually nothing from the 1–1.5mg per 100ml it originally contained. So a dark fridge, and the fresher the better.

A tad indulgent, perhaps, but I rarely keep a bottle past two days of opening, even if it has a week to go on the label. Once open its body clock starts ticking, being surprisingly delicate despite its fairly lengthy shelf life. Also, the more cream the milk contains, the more likely it is to sour – there is no doubt that skimmed milk stores that much longer. Milk can also be frozen, allowing for the tendency of liquids to expand, and also bearing in mind that it will have the same shelf life once thawed.

Top left: Buttermilk Bottom right, from left to right: semi-skimmed, whole and unpasteurised cow's milk

BUTTER

As with milk, butter can derive from any mammal and you can make it with the cream from cows, goats, sheep, camels and a host of other grazing animals. By churning cream we reverse the order, in chemist-speak, from an oil-in-water emulsion to a water-in-oil one. In practice, churning separates the butterfat from the buttermilk, which is what we are left with once we have extracted our prize.

Artisanal butter

In rural Normandy, for the small farmer, the process of making butter builds up during the week, with evenings spent separating cream in the dairy, until there is enough to merit churning. This process of collecting cream over a period of days results in a natural fermentation, which produces certain compounds that give these butters their intensely creamy lactic flavour. Naturally occurring bacteria in the cream convert some of the sugar lactose, to lactic acid, so that it sours slightly.

In Continental European commercial dairies, this process is likely to be helped along. First the cream will be separated from the skimmed milk by means of a centrifuge, then pasteurised and inoculated with the addition of lactic cultures such as *Lactococcus lactis* to ferment or ripen the cream. This ripening is the crucial stage that sets Continental butter apart from others. Nothing compares to a lactic butter; if mountain breezes could be turned into a flavour, this would be it.

But back to the break of dawn on a Norman farm, most likely the day before market, when the collected cream is poured into a barrel, or *baratte*, and simply churned or agitated, probably for about 1–1¼ hours. During this time butter granules form, increase in size and start to cling together until by the end there is a semi-solid mass of butter and the by-product, buttermilk, is then siphoned off from the base of the barrel. After washing, the butter is spread out on a table and shaped into pats with the assistance of two wooden paddles or 'Scotch hands'.

Commercial butter will be made up of about 80% butterfat, while artisanal butters may only contain 65% – if you look closely at their grain as you cut into them, you can see traces of moisture where the beads have joined together. It is always a pleasure to encounter this particular detail indicating, as it does, the quality. The speed at which an old-fashioned churn rotates, compared to a modern powered steel drum, is the difference between a horse and cart and a fast car.

Seasonality

A good butter, like milk and cream, will reflect the season; in Normandy, for instance, the very best derives from grass-fed cattle in May to June, when the pasture is at its richest and the butter its most yellow. Butter certainly shouldn't require the addition of colouring, and I would be very sceptical if you think this is the case.

Buttermilk

The name is a give-away of the product, the liquid left over from making butter. Light and very slightly sour tasting owing to the ripening of the cream prior to churning, in the seventeenth and eighteenth centuries buttermilk would have been one of the dairymaid's perks, and was enjoyed by the rest of society too. These days, for those still making butter on an artisanal basis, it is more likely that the cows benefit.

What we can buy as 'cultured buttermilk' is just that, a manufactured product something like a thin yogurt, made using skimmed milk and cultures specific to the butter-making process. It has long provided the rise in soda bread, by reacting with sodium bicarbonate to produce carbon dioxide, which acts as a leavening agent. It is also enjoying a comeback as an ingredient in dressings and puddings.

A taste of butter

In Europe's thriving local markets, you find butters as different in character as their small producers. There are also regional differences, butters of such quality and character that their names are protected by identifying their geographical origins: the French *Beurre d'Isigny, Beurre Charentes-Poitou* (my all-time favourite) and *Beurre de Deux-Sèvres;* Spain's *Mantequilla de Soria*; and the *Beurre Rose* of Luxembourg.

'C'est un goût'

The flipside to those mountain breezes are the regions where it is not uncommon for artisanal butters to taste pungent, some competing with Stilton for sheer bravado. In Normandy, for instance, If you put this to the seller, you are likely to be dismissed with a Gallic shrug; *'c'est un goût',* meaning 'it's a certain taste', is the usual response to puckering up on being offered a sliver of a particularly pungent farmhouse butter in a market.

The French are not alone in this taste. Spiced Moroccan clarified butter, *smen*, which is buried in the ground and aged for months, even years, must acquire certain odours in the process. Now and again in Ireland some ancient block of butter is unearthed from a peat bog. And the buttered tea prized in the Himalayan regions of Tibet, Bhutan and Nepal is made using rancid yak butter and salt. Again, *'un goût'* to acquire.

Storage and shelf life

An artisanal butter made from unpasteurised cream will have a comparatively short shelf life, around ten days for unsalted and three weeks for salted, compared to commercial butters, which should last for a few months. Before the advent of spreadable butters, it was the norm to keep butter out of the fridge in a covered butter dish, either in a cold corner of your kitchen or a pantry. But this was when you reached for it at every meal and snack opportunity to spread on your bread, and the way we eat has changed. So, if you are only using it occasionally and more as a flavouring or to finish a dish, then the fridge is the best place. And an airtight container helps to ward off unwanted odours.

Originally, butter was salted to help preserve it, whereas today the main consideration is flavour. Given that our butter is chilled, preservation is not such an issue. Unfortunately however, brining is the norm, which tends to make for a metallic aftertaste. Normandy and Brittany fly the flag for salted butters, where there is a thriving tradition of lacing unsalted butter with coarse sea salt. This combines the full creamy lactic hit of a Continental butter with unexpected little crystals of salt that dissolve and flavour whatever you are eating. It makes a treat of steamed veggies and potatoes, perhaps bolstered with some olive oil. I like to have a small 125g pat in the fridge in addition to unsalted butter – it lasts for an age. It is also easy enough to make your own (see page 54).

Spreadable butters

While it may be fine to keep a spreadable butter in the fridge for those impromptu cracker moments, for cooking beware. The vast majority achieve their fridge-to-bread spreadability by the addition of vegetable oil, and will turn sludgy at room temperature. The exception are those that are naturally soft, achieved by skimming a particular layer off a vat of butter, or adjusting the cattle's feed. The Président brand is one of note.

How to cook with butter

As it is the flavour we want, my preferred route when frying is to combine butter with olive or rapeseed oil. This has the double advantage of reducing the saturated fat, while raising the smoke point (the temperature at which it starts to burn and release potentially harmful compounds). It is also usual to fry with unsalted as salted burns more readily.

But frying is one of the more surprising reprieves for butter of late. Sunflower and corn oil are high in polyunsaturates and have long been promoted as the healthy option when frying at comparatively high temperatures of around 180°C. However, when oils and fats are heated their structure changes as they oxidise to form lipid peroxides and, more importantly aldehydes, which even in small quantities have been linked to heart disease and cancer. Tests have revealed that oils high in polyunsaturates create very high levels of toxic aldehydes, whereas the saturated fats such as butter create far fewer, hardly undergoing this oxidisation at all. So frying in saturated fats is potentially healthier than using corn or sunflower oil.

Clarified butter

The milk solids in butter burn at a comparatively low temperature (around 150°C), a problem many chefs overcome by clarifying their butter. You melt it, skim off the surface foam and decant the now-clear butterfat below, discarding the milky solids on the base. In this way you raise the smoke point to about 200°C.

Ghee, the Indian version of clarified butter, takes the process a step further by slowly colouring the milk solids before removing the butter, which adds flavour and helps to prevent rancidity. But, given that it tends to be used as you might olive oil, it's not the healthiest cooking medium as a default.

CHEESE

Travelling back in time a few millennia and cheese fulfilled the role of preserving milk, which deteriorates rapidly in the absence of pasteurisation and chilling. As a concentrated food source it was of huge value, especially if you consider its shelf life compared to, say, fresh meat. Fast forward to today when preservation is no longer such an issue, and increasingly our preference is for young, fresh cheeses, which have the advantage of being lower in both salt and fat than longer-keeping hard cheeses. Such curd cheeses may be made for eating fresh for just a few days, whereas a harder rich cheese like Parmesan can mature for several years.

On the health front, cheeses range from green light to amber and red, principally according to their fat content, although they can also harbour a considerable dose of salt. Trying to ascertain quite what these values are, however, can be a challenge, since labelling and cheeses have conflicting interests. While the supermarket soap-like blocks of industrially produced cheese will provide a nutrient breakdown on the packaging with everything you need to know bar the name of the cow, many of the best cheeses are either artisanal or produced in small quantities, such as you might find in a market or a small independent outlet, where this information will be scarce. With this in mind, the following pointers are intended to give you independence over labelling so that you can simply look at a cheese and know more or less how much fat and salt it is likely to contain.

Traffic lights

The venerable creator of the British Cheese Awards, New Zealander Juliet Harbutt, faced with the infinite variety of cheeses and the confusion that it created for entrants and judges alike, devised an ingenious system for classifying them according to their rind type. In so doing, she came up with seven categories, each one corresponding to a particular band of fat content. These seven categories, in turn, can be grouped further into low-, medium-, high- and very-high-fat cheeses.

It is an incredibly useful little tool for when we are out shopping, and perhaps wondering where on the scale a cheese might lie, especially if it involves a market or small producer where the nutrient content isn't available. As Juliet explains, 'The rind of a cheese tells you a great deal about what's beneath, and with a little experience, you can determine the basic character of all but a handful of cheeses, from its strength of flavour to its age and even its condition.' How so? Because of the moisture within the cheese, which not only accounts for the texture but the type of rind it will develop too.

We can take this one step further with a bit of elementary number-crunching to calculate how much saturated fat a cheese might contain. As a rule of thumb, saturated fat accounts for about two-thirds of the total fat value. So if a cheese has 30g of fat per 100g, you can assume there will be around 20g of saturated fat. When creating your own recipes, you can therefore make a quick recce of how much to add in the interests of health (see opposite).

LOW FAT 22% and below	MEDIUM FAT 22–28%	HIGH FAT 28–36%	VERY HIGH FAT 36% and above

Fresh Cheeses
(no rind)
 	
ricotta
fresh goat's cheese
mozzarella
Burrata
feta
quark
	Aged Fresh Cheeses
	(wrinkled white to
	grey-blue rind)
	
	Soft White Rind
	Cheeses (white
	fuzzy rind)
	
	Semi-soft Cheeses
	(fine to thick
	grey-brown rind or
	orange and sticky)
	
	Camembert
	brie
	Crottin de Chavignol
	raclette
	Saint-Nectaire
	Saint-Félicien
	Chaource
	Livarot
	La Tur
	Gorgonzola
	Vacherin Mont d'Or
	Mimolette (jeune)
	Époises de
	  Bourgogne
		Hard Cheeses
		(dense, and often
		waxed or oily rind)
		
		Blue (gritty,
		rough, sometimes
		sticky rind)
		
		Emmental
		cheddar
		Abondance
		Mimolette (vieille)
		Gouda
		Roquefort
		Cantal
		Tête de Moine
		Tomme de Brebis
		Leerdammer
		Parmesan
			Soft White Rind
			Cheeses with
			added cream
			(white fuzzy rind)
			Cream Cheeses
			
			mascarpone
			Délice de
			  Bourgogne
			blue goat's cheese

When in Europe

To complicate our lives, on the Continent of Europe, classification sometimes takes the form of 'fat and dry matter'. As its name suggests, this is where the water content of the cheese has been extracted to ascertain how much fat remains within the residual dry matter, and it pushes the figure way up. Most cheeses (unless they have had cream added) will contain under 45% fat, so should you happen to encounter a cheese – brie and Camembert in particular – that sports some ludicrously high fat content such as 75%, chances are this form of classification will go to explain why. So don't be put off buying it.

Salt

Salt is a sensitive issue: essential to life and yet potentially fatal. Sodium regulates fluid balance, and is crucial for the transmission of nerve and muscle impulses. Too much over a period of time, however, and it will raise our blood pressure and place us at risk of cardiovascular disease, as well as increasing our chances of developing stomach cancer, and sodium is linked to kidney disease. We could certainly exist on a great deal less than the majority of us are accustomed to consuming: the average intake exceeds the recommendation of a maximum of 6g a day, when 1g would suffice for normal physiological function.

It is not always easy to work out how much salt we are eating, given that 80% of the salt that we consume is already contained in the food we buy (most of this comes from bread), and labelling is less than transparent. From a labelling perspective, it is worth noting that salt is made up of 40% sodium and 60% chloride, and frequently the value for sodium will be quoted, which you need to multiply by 2.5 in order to attain the value for salt. Without taking this on board, it is both logical and easy to look at the sodium value and think you are consuming less salt than the reality.

There can be no separating salt from mature cheeses where it acts as a processing aid that assists fermentation. And brining cheese not only results in a lovely washed rind but it provides a medium for feta and other curd cheeses of that style.

Yet another set of traffic lights

The traffic light system gives a green light to cheese with a salt content below 0.3g per 100 g, an amber light to 0.3–1.5g and a red light above 1.5g. Cheese can range from zero salt content for fresh yogurt-style cheeses, to being red light, which is characteristic of hard mature cheeses. This doesn't mean don't eat them, the trick is simply to consider the total value of salt in whatever you are cooking. If you are going to add some Parmesan to a risotto, bear in mind its salt content when seasoning the dish. Likewise, many salads and vegetable dishes may be able to forego any additional salt if you are including it as an ingredient, or perhaps making a blue cheese dressing. So it is a case of lateral thinking.

Cooking with cheese

I grew up against a backdrop of fondues, gratins and dishes like cauliflower cheese, all of which push the limits on fat (and energy) to a point where they are less than wholesome. The good news is the transition to today's style and the enjoyment of cheese in a much broader and more creative way than twenty or thirty years ago. And cheese is perhaps most successfully incorporated in a cameo role. A dusting of Parmesan over a bowl of soup, or just a little gruyère, Abondance, Emmental or Comté scattered over a vegetable bake or added to a salad will contribute character and luxury without crossing any red lines.

A medium-mature goat's cheese is a staple in my fridge, for crumbling into a salad of roast vegetables and spelt, into muffins, omelettes and frittatas. While lower-fat cheeses – those with a high protein content that are curd-like in character and hold their shape, such as ricotta – are ideal for fillings and for scattering over dishes to be grilled, and quark and fromage frais come into their own for sweet dishes where you want something tender and creamy.

Top left: Abondance **Top right:** Fresh goat's cheese **Bottom left:** La Tur **Bottom right** Tomme de Brebis

CREAM

If I had to choose one ingredient that defines change in the way we cook from a couple of decades ago, it would be cream. My childhood was characterised by Billy Bunter-esque lashings of double cream that drowned gorgeous hot fluffy sponge puddings and crumbles, was whipped to soft peaks for a thick crowning blanket on a trifle and used to offset the saccharine marshmallow meringue of a lemon meringue pie. Single? I am ashamed to say it stood in for milk when we had run out of that for coffee and tea, and cornflakes with banana were vastly improved with a tub on the table.

It is hard to put the eschewing of such habits down to any one particular factor. Health undeniably, but I would also add the arrival of crème fraîche and with it a less-is-more approach. This cream has real flavour, and for me has proved the game-changer. A small teaspoon with chocolate cake suffices where previously a small jug of the stuff was called for. It is also endlessly adaptable; if you are going to have just one tub in the fridge, this is it.

A RICH VARIETY

Single
With a fat content of 19% (12% saturated), this is the lightest cream. It has a thin pouring consistency – a drop makes a good addition to a soup at the end of cooking, warmed through without boiling. And if you are making a mousse or dessert that you are setting with gelatine, then it is an astute choice over and above a richer cream.

Whipping
With a fat content of 40% (25% saturated), the advantage of whipping cream lies in being the lowest in fat for whisking to aerated fluffy peaks.

Frequently I will combine whipped cream with a low-fat Greek yogurt. Where the latter is too austere and heavy on its own in a dessert, just a little whipping cream will provide that luxurious savour as well as lightening it.

Double
This comes in at a hefty 54% fat (33% saturated), but its greatest sin is a relative lack of flavour. For that amount of saturated fat it is fair to expect a bit more bang for your bucks. Save it for the occasional trickle in a soup or over a dessert. (The extra-thick version is double cream that has been preheated and then rapidly cooled, which accounts for its thickness.)

Soured cream
I turn to soured cream more and more because, with half the fat of crème fraîche or the same amount as single cream, it is brilliant for enriching all manner of dips, sauces and dressings. It works best in savoury dishes, though, whereas crème fraîche is equally at home in savoury or sweet. But unlike crème fraîche, which is dependable under the duress of heat, soured cream tends to split, so it is best added cold.

Crème fraîche

Despite its heavy and unctuous texture, the fat content of crème fraîche is on a par with whipping cream. It is made by maturing pasteurised cream for about 18 hours with lactic starters, which cause it to develop the particular flavour and characteristic acidities of butter. It keeps for weeks, and it is heat stable, so a great one for simmering in sauces and the like without having to fret that it might renege and split.

The low-fat version of crème fraîche, however, is to be avoided. Most usually this is thickened with the help of stabilisers and xanthan gum. Better to go for soured cream.

Crème crue

Gorgeously thick and sticky, and a pale ivory, raw unpasteurised cream is very similar to crème fraîche. It ripens naturally rather than with the addition of cultures. I tend to use it instead of crème fraîche when I am in Normandy where I can buy it from markets and local shops. Crème crue is a niche product, but you might come across it in farm shops.

Clotted

Clotted cream has the double accolade of being the most interesting and characterful of creams at the same time as being the richest. I'm not sure we really want to know the fat content of clotted cream, otherwise we would never buy it again, and it is far too good to cold shoulder. But in the interests of transparency, it weighs in at about 64% fat (40% saturated). That is quite a feat, not stopping short of butter. An occasional treat, or just a small spoonful.

This indulgence originates in the West Country, Cornwall and Devon, where a farmhouse cream tea is still the highlight of a long weekend or holiday. Traditionally, the cream is scalded until it forms a golden crust, and then skimmed from the surface leaving the milk below. Thick and sticky, the cream gets thin towards the bottom. It has a unique granular texture, and a faintly caramelised flavour courtesy of the milk sugars that have cooked.

Top right: A selection of creams Bottom left: Crème fraîche and soured cream

How to Cook with Cream

In terms of reliability, the higher the percentage of butterfat, the more heat-friendly a cream becomes. This is because the fat globules are pulling rank over the protein, making it less likely to split in the presence of lemon juice or vinegar, and very salty foods. Equally, it is unlikely to form a skin when heated.

This results in a clear sliding scale, with single cream at the lower end, capricious and likely to split if simmered, to whipping, which is more stable, while double cream (at the top end) is pretty much foolproof, as is crème fraîche. Soured cream, however, which contains less butterfat than crème fraîche, can, like single cream, curdle if cooked. It is fine to add soured cream to a soup or sauce at the end to warm through, but I wouldn't recommend boiling or simmering vigorously, or it tends to 'bead'.

Whisking

Whipping cream is a useful partner to lower-fat dairy products such as ricotta, quark or low-fat Greek yogurt for puds, in which case you may want to whisk it first. The slight disadvantage is the way it can liquefy at the base after a few hours, although it can be rewhisked. If you are setting a pud with gelatine, then this is less of an issue, and whipping makes a good choice for a lighter mousse. It is best to add sugar towards the end to maximise the volume.

The one proviso when whisking cream is the external temperature. During a hot summer, cream will do its own thing and turn to butter at the sight of a whisk. So this is something to bear in mind. Watch the tennis instead.

Storage

Store creams in the coldest section of the fridge, and be guided by their use-by dates. If you are an infrequent user, however, the best keepers are crème fraîche and soured cream.

YOGURT

The diversity of yogurt is magnified immensely if you consider that it is nothing more than milk and bacteria; a small beginning for the plethora of yogurt styles ranging from thin and sharp to voluptuously thick and creamy, and this is before we start exploring flavoured and other types. Keep in mind simplicity of origin when you buy, and avoid the mass of flavourings, gelling agents, preservatives, sweeteners or sugar that are no improvement on the real thing and so often a short cut to the desired character.

Yogurt is characterised by its sharp taste, and this is down to the bacterial fermentation of milk, where cultures ferment lactose, the naturally occurring sugar in milk, to lactic acid. A typical starter culture might contain *Lactobacillus bulgaricus, L. acidophilus* and *Streptococcus thermophilus*. You need not get too close to these little guys, but it is useful to know the mechanics. And for many producers, the precise blend is classified information. There are also regional species and strains of bacteria, which give rise to local specialities, Greek and Bulgarian, for example.

The key word when buying is 'live', which indicates that the yogurt contains active bacteria. Those advertised as containing probiotics have live probiotic bacteria, which may be beneficial to health. Bio yogurts have specific strains of bacteria, such as *Bifidobacterium bifidum* or *B. longum and/or Lactobacillus acidophilus*, that make for a milder and creamier yogurt.

The character of a yogurt depends on the type of milk it is made with. Cow's is the most common, but sheep's and goat's milks make for lovely creamy yogurts, and there are other regional varieties – water buffalo, camel, yak? The temperature and duration of fermentation, and whether or not it has been strained, all play a part in the style of the finished product.

Greek yogurt
Strained to remove some of the water content (the whey), like fromage frais Greek yogurt can range from 0% fat to 8–10%. Zero-fat has a similar profile to low-fat quark: with double the protein and half the carbohydrate of a 'virtually fat-free yogurt' that is thin and insipid by comparison, it is small wonder that the various strained versions have gained such a following.

I tend to use 0%-fat Greek yogurt and quark interchangeably, although the quark does have a definite sense of being a curd cheese rather than a yogurt. This aside, both are young, fresh and delightful. They are also a good choice for those who find the stronger lactic taste of some natural yogurts off-putting.

There is, however, a world of difference between Greek and Greek-style yogurt, following a lengthy legal battle. The real thing has a protected status. The pretenders, made elsewhere, tend to be a rich classic yogurt, tarter in flavour and thinner. So unless a recipe specifies Greek-style, genuine Greek yogurt is usually superior.

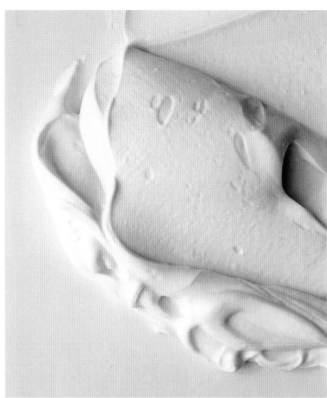

Top left: Yogurt-making equipment Top right: Quark Bottom left: Yogurts

Fromage frais

This is a young, fresh cheese that originates from northern France and southern Belgium. Ever creamy, even 0%-fat tastes substantially richer than a fat-free yogurt and less sharp. Fromage frais and fromage blanc tend to be sold interchangeably, even though technically they differ. Fromage frais must contain live cultures at the point of sale, whereas with fromage blanc fermentation has been halted. One speciality worth looking out for is fromage frais *à la faisselle*, which refers to the mould in which it is strained. Perfect whenever you want a curd cheese to play with, it is sharper and has a *pétillant* effect, a lively hint of fizz that tastes peppery on the tongue.

Quark

This German soft fresh curd cheese has recently taken the chill cabinet by storm, beyond its place of origin. In Germany, it comes in many different forms and levels of fat, but it is the low-fat type that has put down roots elsewhere in the world. It is fab stuff, whether you want something for breakfast with berries or for using in a cheesecake. It has a very high protein content, which makes it the beloved choice of many low-carbers. Hard to imagine how we ever did without this one. As with Greek yogurt, it is worth seeking an authentic German quark, rather than a copy.

How to cook with yogurt

The criticism sometimes levelled at low-fat yogurts and their ilk is the trade-off of flavour for health. Certainly standard yogurts can be insipid, whereas a low-fat Greek yogurt has all the texture, and provides an ideal foundation for enriching in a way that suits your taste. That could be achieved by combining it with a little soured cream or crème fraîche, or just a drizzle of single or whipping cream, or olive oil. In this way you get the best of both worlds, the requisite luxury without the higher fat content of richer products.

Most of the recipes that follow will use these products cold. If they are included in a hot dish, then I try to avoid simmering to risk them splitting and add them at the end.

LACTOSE INTOLERANCE

An intolerance to lactose (hypolactasia), which may result in unwanted but rarely serious symptoms, differs from an allergy, which is potentially injurious. And different people can have different levels of intolerance. Some may not be able to digest so much as a tablespoon of milk without regret, while others will be able to cope with a larger amount, especially if consumed in the presence of other food.

The majority of the lactose intolerant still produce some of the enzyme lactase and can deal with a small amount of lactose: some research suggests up to 12g of lactose in a single sitting (about one glass of milk). But for the recipes that follow that are marked as lactose-free (LF), I have set the level at a trace of 1g per 100ml or less, which will accommodate all but extreme intolerance.

It is also possible that, if you think you may be sensitive to dairy, by giving it a miss for some time and then gradually re-introducing it, your body may overcome any sensitivity.

A GLOBAL PERSPECTIVE

If you are affected, you are far from alone. It wasn't until the 1960s that medical experts realised the inability to digest lactose beyond infancy is in fact the norm rather than the exception. Around 70% of Africans and Asians are lactose intolerant, although this can rise to almost 100% in certain countries, compared to 5–15% of Northern Europeans who have adapted to the inclusion of animal milk products in their diet by continuing to produce the enzyme lactase beyond weaning. There is one story, apocryphal maybe, of a hundred Asians being offered the choice of either eating a spider or a cube of cheddar. Seventy-five chose the spider. One hypothesis is that the people of central and northern Europe, where distance from the equator means fewer hours of daylight, particularly during the winter months, have adapted genetically to prolong natural production of lactase, enabling them to continue to consume milk-based products and benefit from the calcium and vitamin content.

WHAT IS LACTOSE INTOLERANCE?

At birth, we all derive something like 40% of our energy from the lactose present in breast milk, the principal carbohydrate in our diet during these early days. The milk sugar lactose is a disaccharide that has to be broken down into its constituent monosaccharide units, glucose and galactose, in the small intestine, in order to be metabolised as precious energy for the body.

However, for much of the global population, the body rationalises that, as it no longer needs the lactase for breast milk, it will stop producing it. This is when the trouble begins, as the undigested sugar passes into the colon. Here fermentation produces the bloating and stomach pain that we associate with intolerance. This is known as primary lactose intolerance. Some individuals suffering from IBS also link their symptoms to dairy; at least 25% of those suffering from IBS also have lactose malabsorption. And, there is a more severe form, known as secondary lactose intolerance, which presents as a reduction of lactase caused by diseases of the intestinal tract, protein-energy malnutrition, intestinal infections and coeliac disease.

SO WHAT DAIRY CAN YOU EAT?

Curds not whey
Lactose is water-soluble, so any curdling process that precipitates out the curds results in most of the lactose being contained within the whey.

Butter
Butter contains only a small amount of milk solids and is therefore comparatively free of lactose. Clarified butter and ghee, however, are lactose-free, as the milk solids have been removed. This represents the safest route to including butter in your diet if you know that you are highly sensitive to this sugar.

Cheese
With cheeses, where possible check the label. The only sugar to be found in pure dairy products (those without the addition of fruit or other ingredients) will be lactose, which will be listed as the carbohydrate value. So immediately you have a gauge as to how much lactose the product contains.

Mature cheeses like Gouda, gruyère and cheddar, and also Camembert and brie contain only traces of lactose, whereas whey-based cheeses such as ricotta, cottage cheese and quark are unsuitable. As a rule of thumb, if the cheese seems very wet, or oozes a small amount of liquid, then it is likely to contain some of the whey.

Yogurt
Research has revealed an interesting anomaly with yogurt and lactose intolerance, illustrated by the culture of consuming yogurt in many Asian countries where the population is otherwise lactose sensitive. In India, for example, there is a rich tradition of yogurt drinks and raitas, and it is widely used for cooking. Research has provided several theories to explain why it is that people with a low production of lactase can better tolerate the lactose in yogurt than that in milk. This could be due to the activity of live bacteria in the yogurt or the digestive action of other enzymes on the lactose, but possibly also because the increased viscosity of yogurt makes for a longer transit time through the gastrointestinal tract that may reduce the amount of lactose present in the colon. Either way, yogurt is well tolerated by those who struggle with milk and other dairy products. But ultimately this is down to trial and error on the part of the individual.

HOMEMADE

Yogurt-making

I came to yogurt-making as a novice at the start of writing this book. Why make it when it is so readily available? And during the initial stages of trying my hand I remained sceptical – especially since many recipes recommended using UHT milk with skimmed milk powder. This led to a pact: unless I could devise a system that was foolproof and as good as or better than anything I could buy, I would pass on my apologies and leave it out.

So when I eventually came up with a yogurt that stood proud next to anything I have tasted from a chill cabinet, it felt like a giant leap. And the basic is only the beginning. From there we can travel to so many places – to strawberry and raspberry yogurt, spicy treacle, apple and raisin to Greek-style yogurt, fromage frais and quark. It rewrites the potential of any number of recipes that follow.

Cheat just a little

Most introductions to making your own yogurt kick off with 'you don't need a yogurt maker', so I realise I am bucking the trend here. Homemade yogurt is inclined to be a tad hair-shirt; that is, for the resourceful you could either nurse it like a baby in the warm environs of an airing cupboard, or be creative with a Thermos flask. But how many people have airing cupboards? And while some Thermos flasks may cruise along at an even ambient temperature overnight, others go into a downward spiral of heat loss as soon as they are stoppered. Certainly, they cannot promise the stable temperature beloved of yogurt-making bacteria over a prescribed period of time.

The notion of buying a dedicated machine to make something this simple may seem a bit feeble. But there again, we can boil water in a saucepan, which doesn't stop us buying electric kettles. So yes, making yogurt is elementary, but it is also a finely tuned process that relies on a nurturing warm ambience being sustained over a long period of time. And since it's the same price as that kettle (or rather less, see suppliers, page 189), and a machine that will take up no more room than the thermos, there is every reason to follow this path. I would recommend a maker in the form of a single large tub, rather than little pots, as most of the recipes here involve straining or flavouring the yogurt, so you will need to decant it first.

Timing

The timing of making yogurt has everything to do with how much sleep you like getting at night. If it's seven hours or under, then you could set the yogurt going before turning in for the night, and chill it the following morning ready for lunch. While for those who like in excess of seven hours (*moi*), the best route is to make it during the day and chill it overnight.

Culture

Any yogurt with live bacteria is suitable for making yogurt at home. Simply choose a commercial yogurt with a style that you like and your resulting yogurt should mirror its qualities. As a fan of Total Greek yogurt, I frequently turn to this one; both the full-fat and the 0%-fat versions are suitable. Otherwise, an organic natural yogurt is a good route (see page 34 for more on cultures).

Milk

Both whole and semi-skimmed milk will make lovely creamy yogurts, but skimmed milk is best reserved for straining to make quark (see page 46). If making a strained Greek-style yogurt, you will end up with about half yogurt and half whey and will be doubling the fat content of the milk.

*A yogurt made using whole milk with about 4% butterfat will be about 8% fat, similar to the richest fromage frais; a semi-skimmed milk about 4% fat, while a skimmed milk one will be 0%.

YOGURT – THE BASIC RECIPE

Makes approx. 700g

900ml whole milk (see below)*
2 teaspoons live yogurt

1. Bring the milk almost to the boil in a medium–large saucepan (the milk is likely to catch and burn in the corners of a small pan). The surface should be trembling with small bubbles, and might have formed a skin.

2. Pour it into a large bowl and leave it to cool to just below 50°C (about 48°C). I use a jam thermometer to measure this. Left to its own accord this will take around 20–30 minutes, but can be speeded up by pouring the hot milk into a second bowl, as you might cool hot food to be fed to an impatient young child by transferring it from one cold plate to another. Now pass it through a sieve to remove any skin that has formed.

3. About 5 minutes before the end of cooling the milk, turn on the heated component of your yogurt maker. Spoon the yogurt into the inner bowl, add about a mug of the hot milk and whisk to blend, then add the remaining milk and whisk again to blend these. Place this bowl within the incubator.

4. Put the lid on, cover with the outer lid and leave for 6 hours. My own preference is for a yogurt that is nicely set but on the gentle side. If you like a distinctive tart flavour, then you can leave it for a few hours longer.

By this time you should see some whey floating on the surface of the yogurt, which should have set. Leave the inner bowl to cool for about 30 minutes before chilling in the fridge for half a day or overnight.

5. Drain off the whey and give the yogurt a stir. This should leave you with a classic yogurt with a slightly grainy appearance.

SOURCE OF VIT B2, CALCIUM, PHOSPHOROUS, IODINE
(per 100g, see page 46) Energy 79 Kcal | Fat 3g | Sat fat 1.9g | Carbs 7.8g | Sugar 7.8g | Protein 5.7g | Salt 0.1g

STRAINED GREEK-STYLE YOGURT

My preference is for a rich, creamy Greek-style of yogurt, achieved by straining. Aside from its luxurious texture, I find tart yogurts too reminiscent of sour milk (the memory of the crate of bottles of milk at school left warming on a doorstep for a few hours before they were handed out at breaktime) and straining off the whey modifies that element. There is no need for additional cream because you will be enriching the yogurt naturally. A whole milk yogurt will be that much creamier than one made using semi-skimmed milk (see 'milk' opposite).

Makes approx. 350g

700g homemade yogurt (see above)

1. Set a sieve over a large bowl and line it with a double thickness of kitchen paper. Tip the yogurt into the sieve and loosely cover with clingfilm, then return to the fridge for half a day to drain. At the end of this time you should have a thick, slightly grainy yogurt and the same volume of whey – the clear greenish liquid in the bowl.

2. Tip the strained yogurt into a food processor (the kitchen paper should peel off with ease), and whizz until smooth and creamy. Your yogurt is now ready to eat plain, or to flavour (see page 45).

SOURCE OF CALCIUM, PHOSPHOROUS, IODINE
(per 100g, see page 46) Energy 133 Kcal | Fat 10.2g | Sat fat 6.8g | Carbs 4.8g | Sugar 4.5g | Protein 5.7g | Salt 0.1g

FLAVOURED YOGURTS

Using 350g strained Greek-style yogurt (see the basic recipe on page 43)

VANILLA

1 teaspoon vanilla bean paste
15g golden caster sugar

Blend all the ingredients with the yogurt and leave to stand for 5–10 minutes for the sugar to dissolve, before stirring and dividing between small pots. Cover and chill.

SOURCE OF CALCIUM, PHOSPHOROUS, IODINE
(per 100g) Energy 144 Kcal | Fat 9.8g | Sat fat 6.5g | Carbs 8.5g | Sugar 8.2g | Protein 5.4g | Salt 0.2g

STRAWBERRY OR RASPBERRY

75g ripe strawberries (hulled weight) or raspberries
15g golden caster sugar

Coarsely mash the strawberries or raspberries with the sugar in a bowl, then blend with the yogurt and leave to stand for 5–10 minutes for the sugar to dissolve, before stirring and dividing between small pots. Cover and chill.

SOURCE OF VIT C, PHOSPHOROUS, IODINE
(per 100g) Energy 124 Kcal | Fat 8.1g | Sat fat 5.4g | Carbs 8g | Sugar 7.8g | Protein 4.6g | Salt 0.1g

SPICY TREACLE

½ teaspoon black treacle
15g golden caster sugar
⅓ teaspoon ground ginger or cinnamon

Blend all the ingredients with the yogurt and leave to stand for 5–10 minutes for the sugar to dissolve, before stirring and dividing between small pots. Cover and chill.

SOURCE OF CALCIUM, PHOSPHOROUS, IODINE
(per 100g) Energy 145 Kcal | Fat 9.7g | Sat fat 6.4g | Carbs 9.2g | Sugar 8.8g | Protein 5.4g | Salt 0.2g

APPLE AND GOJI BERRY OR RAISIN

1 apple, peeled and coarsely grated
15g goji berries or raisins
1 generous tablespoon runny honey
toasted almonds or chopped hazelnuts, to serve (optional)

Stir the apple and goji berries or raisins into the yogurt, drizzle over the honey and turn over a few times to streak it. Serve scattered with nuts if wished.

SOURCE OF PHOSPHOROUS, IODINE
(per 100g) Energy 136 Kcal | Fat 7.8g | Sat fat 5.1g | Carbs 12g | Sugar 11.7g | Protein 4.4g | Salt 0.1g

LABNA

Makes approx. 275g

Blend 350g Greek yogurt (either homemade strained whole milk yogurt, see page 43, or Total natural Greek yogurt) with 1 tablespoon each of finely chopped mint, chives and flat-leaf parsley and 1/4 teaspoon of salt. Tip this into a fine-mesh sieve (or one lined with a clean tea towel) set over a large bowl, loosely cover with clingfilm and chill for 24 hours. You can either use the labna as a cream cheese spread or, if it is firm enough, using your hands roll it into balls the size of a cherry. Arrange these in a shallow dish and pour over some extra virgin olive oil. This is delicious served with toasted sourdough, bresaola and watercress.

SOURCE OF VIT A, CALCIUM, PHOSPHOROUS, IODINE
(per 100g) Energy 129 Kcal | Fat 9.9g | Sat fat 6.5g | Carbs 4.5g | Sugar 4.2g | Protein 5.5g | Salt 0.5g

QUARK

Makes approx. 300g

For a product closely resembling quark, make a skimmed milk yogurt as on page 43, strain it for 2 hours and then whizz in a food processor. It will set a little after a few hours chilling. Even though this is technically a yogurt since it contains live cultures, in keeping with a low-fat quark it has 0% fat, and is high in protein.

SOURCE OF VITS B2, B12, CALCIUM, PHOSPHOROUS, FOLATE
(per 100g)* Energy 74 Kcal | Fat 0g | Sat fat 0g | Carbs 4g | Sugar 4g | Protein 14.6g | Salt 0.1g

CREAM CHEESE

Makes approx. 225g

For a really beautiful cream cheese, that is both unsalted and lighter than anything you can buy, make a whole milk yoghurt as on page 43, then continue to make a Greek-style of yoghurt. Now strain this a second time, for 24 hours in the same fashion.

HIGH IN VITAMIN A
(per 100g)* Energy 439 Kcal | Fat 47.4g | Sat fat 29.7g | Carbs 0g | Sugar 0g | Protein 3.1g | Salt 0.7g

FROMAGE FRAIS

I have long held a soft spot for fromage frais, sweet and gentle, even the low- or 0%-fat versions will stand in for cream, so devising a way to make it at home is high on the list.

Makes approx. 250g

900ml whole milk
2 teaspoons fromage frais

1. Use the basic method for making yogurt on page 43. You can use skimmed, semi-skimmed or whole milk (see 'milk' on page 42). The only difference is to mature it for longer, 12 hours as opposed to 6 hours.

2. Chill the fromage frais for a couple of hours before straining it for a further 2 hours. Instead of whizzing it in a food processor, carefully tip the contents of the sieve into a medium bowl and whisk until smooth and creamy.

SOURCE OF VIT B12, PHOSPHOROUS
(per 100g)* Energy 113 Kcal | Fat 8g | Sat fat 5.5g | Carbs 4.4g | Sugar 4.1g | Protein 6.1g | Salt 0.1g

*Nutritional analysis for yogurt (page 43), quark, cream cheese and fromage frais based on the UK Comp. of Foods integrated dataset (CoF IDS) per 100g only.

WHIPPED BUTTERS

If a fridge should be full of handy little accessories, one or two of these has to be high on the wish list. Each has its own charm, and because of their opulent character, you only need a fraction than you might were it butter alone. So here are a few suggestions for using them.

Your butter should be really soft and creamy to begin, so leave it to come up to room temperature and then work it in a small bowl using a spoon until it is light and fluffy. If you want to make up a larger quantity, then an electric whisk is an excellent route to a really pale and mousse-like butter.

SWEET BUTTERS

*Gorgeous slathered over hot toasted bread and muffins or currant buns
*Smear over pancakes or Scotch pancakes
*Dot over a fruit and nut pudding, such as a Christmas pud
*Use to sauté fruits such as pears, apples, peaches, plums and figs
*Lovely for baking apples and other autumnal fruits
*Spread on sliced panettone
*Serve with hot crusty baguette and summer fruits

CHOCOLATE NUT BUTTER

50g unsalted butter, softened
20g dark chocolate (approx. 70% cocoa), finely grated or chopped
20g Brazil or hazelnuts, roasted and finely chopped

Work the butter in a small bowl until soft and creamy, then work in the chocolate and nuts.

HIGH IN VITS A, E, B7, MANGANESE | SOURCE OF IODINE
(per 10g serving) Energy 69 Kcal | Fat 6.8g | Sat fat 3.6g | Carbs 1.4g | Sugar 1.3g | Protein 0.5g | Salt trace

HONEY BUTTER

50g unsalted butter, softened
2 teaspoons set honey

Work the butter in a small bowl until soft and creamy, then add the honey and blend to streak the butter.

HIGH IN VIT A | SOURCE OF IODINE
(per 10g serving) Energy 70 Kcal | Fat 6.9g | Sat fat 4.3g | Carbs 2g | Sugar 2g | Protein 0.1g | Salt trace

DOUBLE GINGER BUTTER

50g unsalted butter, softened
2 teaspoons finely chopped stem ginger
¼ teaspoon ground ginger

Work the butter in a small bowl until soft and creamy, then work in the two gingers.

HIGH IN VIT A | SOURCE OF VIT D, IODINE
(per 10g serving) Energy 95 Kcal | Fat 6.9g | Sat fat 4.3g | Carbs 0.3g | Sugar 0.1g | Protein 0.1g | Salt trace

VANILLA CINNAMON BUTTER

50g unsalted butter, softened
1½ teaspoons vanilla extract
¼ teaspoon ground cinnamon
1 teaspoon maple or agave syrup

Work the butter in a small bowl until soft and creamy, then work in the vanilla and cinnamon. Add the syrup and blend to streak the butter.

HIGH IN VIT A | SOURCE OF VIT D, IODINE
(per 10g serving) Energy 66 Kcal | Fat 6.9g | Sat fat 4.3g | Carbs 0.9g | Sugar 0.8g | Protein 0.1g | Salt trace

Left: Panettone with
Chocolate Nut Butter

SAVOURY BUTTERS

*Dot over lightly boiled or steamed green vegetables

*Add a sliver with a drop of olive oil when sautéing vegetables such as mushrooms, courgettes, asparagus, leeks, peppers or broccoli

*Drop a teaspoon into the centre of a bowl of vegetable soup

*Smear a little over a chicken before roasting, or under the skin

*Spread a little onto croutons for aperitifs

*Use to enrich a vegetable-based sauce such as tomato

*Replace a little of the butter for pastry for a flavoured crust

*Enliven grains with a sliver before serving

*Stir a little into finished risotto

*Use to fry an omelette

TOMATO AND ROSE PETAL BUTTER

50g unsalted butter, softened
2 teaspoons sun-dried tomato paste
½ teaspoon dried rose petals, finely chopped

Work the butter in a small bowl until it is really soft and creamy, then add the tomato paste and rose petals and blend to streak the butter.

HIGH IN VITS A, E | SOURCE OF VIT D, IODINE
(per 10g serving) Energy 70 Kcal | Fat 7.7g | Sat fat 4.5g | Carbs 0.1g | Sugar 0.1g | Protein 0.1g | Salt trace

MISO BUTTER

50g unsalted butter, softened
20g miso

Work the butter in a small bowl until it is really soft and creamy, then add the miso and blend to streak the butter.

HIGH IN VIT A | SOURCE OF IODINE
(per 10g serving) Energy 59 Kcal | Fat 6g | Sat fat 3.7g | Carbs 0.7g | Sugar trace | Protein 0.4g | Salt 0.3g

PIMENT D'ESPELETTE AND LEMON BUTTER

50g salted butter, softened
¼ teaspoon Piment d'Espelette or cayenne pepper
½ teaspoon finely grated lemon zest
squeeze of lemon juice

Work the butter in a small bowl until it is really soft and creamy, then work in the Piment d'Espelette and lemon zest and juice.

HIGH IN VIT A | SOURCE OF VIT D, IODINE
(per 10g serving) Energy 63 Kcal | Fat 6.9g | Sat fat 4.3g | Carbs 0.1g | Sugar 0.1g | Protein 0.1g | Salt trace

ZA'ATAR BUTTER

50g salted butter, softened
1 level teaspoon za'atar
squeeze of lemon juice

Work the butter in a small bowl until it is really soft and creamy, then work in the za'atar and lemon juice.

HIGH IN VIT A | SOURCE OF VIT D, IODINE
(per 10g serving) Energy 63 Kcal | Fat 6.9g | Sat fat 4.3g | Carbs 0.2g | Sugar 0.1g | Protein 0.1g | Salt trace

Right: Tomato and Rose Petal Butter spread on a slice of steamed Romesco

Top left: Garlic Herb Butter with Sourdough **Top right:** Anchovy Butter **Bottom left:** Garlic Herb Butter **Bottom right** Anchovy Toasts with Cavolo Nero

CLASSIC BUTTERS

GARLIC BUTTER

50g salted butter, e.g. Breton or Norman, softened

6 tablespoons soft herbs (a mixture of parsley, chives, chervil, coriander or tarragon), finely chopped

1 garlic clove, peeled and crushed

Work the butter in a medium bowl until it is really soft and creamy, then work in the herbs and garlic.

HIGH IN VITS A, K, C | SOURCE OF IODINE
(per 10g serving) Energy 46 Kcal | Fat 4.9g | Sat fat 3.1g | Carbs 0.3g | Sugar 0.1g | Protein 0.2g | Salt trace

HERB BUTTER

As for garlic butter, omitting the garlic.

GARLIC OR HERB BREAD

Either thickly slice 1 small baguette, leaving the pieces attached at the base, and generously spread either side of each slice (my preferred route), or slit it in half and spread top and bottom, then wrap it up in foil. This can be made a day in advance and chilled.

Bake for 15 minutes at 180°C fan /200°C/gas mark 6, then open up the foil and cook for a further 5 minutes to crisp the crust.

SOURCE OF FIBRE
(per 53g serving) Energy 156 Kcal | Fat 3.3g | Sat fat 1.7g | Carbs 25.8g | Sugar 1.3g | Protein 4.9g | Salt 0.8g

BUTTERED ANCHOVY PASTE

This is a homemade Gentleman's Relish, but gentler. You can slather it onto hot toast with abandon where it will melt louchely over the top, or spread it thinly on cold crisp slivers.

75g salted anchovy fillets

100g unsalted butter, softened

large pinch each of grated nutmeg, ground ginger and ground cinnamon

couple of shakes of Tabasco

Place all the ingredients in a food processor and whizz to a smooth butter. It is delightful eaten straight away while soft and mousse-like, but otherwise pack it into a small pot or jar, seal and chill. It will be good for at least a week.

LF ANCHOVY TOASTS WITH CAVOLO NERO

Serves 6

Cut out the central stalk from 400g cavolo nero and slice or coarsely chop the leaves. Blanch it for 3 minutes in a large pan of salted water, then drain and press out any excess liquid. Toss with 3 tablespoons of extra virgin olive oil and 1 tablespoon of lemon juice, and season with sea salt and black pepper.

Slather the anchovy paste onto shallow slices of coarse-textured white toast and pile with the cavolo nero. Top with a halved quail egg (boiled for 2½ minutes, then shelled), or some chopped hard-boiled egg.

HIGH IN VITS A, K, C, B12 | SOURCE OF FOLATE, CALCIUM
Energy 360 Kcal | Fat 23.8g | Sat fat 10.5g | Carbs 23g | Sugar 2.6g | Protein 11.3g | Salt 2.2g

SALTED BUTTER

Normandy with its *beurre au sel* and *demi-sel* spoils us for all other salted butters. Having been raised on a commercial salted butter (shipped from the other side of the world in the cold store of a ship), I held a long-standing aversion. Its bitter aftertaste and ubiquitous texture come of salting butter with brine made from a chemically treated salt – a far cry from the finesse of a sweet lactic butter laced with sea salt crystals. First encounter in France and it was love. A lactic butter has been ripened or cultured, which gives it an inimitable discreet sour note. Today I wouldn't be without a small pat in the fridge door for the occasional sliver melting over lightly cooked broccoli or asparagus, or mashed potato.

In the dairy of a local farm in Normandy where I buy my supplies, there is a compact chilled room where several women will be in charge of churning and kneading the butter into pats. But the salting, for this family at least, is the domain of *grandpère,* who arrives when the freshly churned butter has been spread out on the table in a thick layer. He takes handfuls of coarse sea salt, *sel gris,* from a tub, and scatters it over the butter as though he were throwing seeds onto freshly ploughed earth.

It is just as easy to make it yourself, in which case you can use any salt of your choosing. I like to use Maldon sea salt, but keep it regional and use whatever salt is particular to the area where you live. These are *grandpère's* recipes. This is also a good occasion to whip the butter if you wish, and while you might only want a flavoured butter in a small quantity, salted butter has many uses and will keep well for weeks.

DEMI-SEL
235g unsalted butter, softened
15g Maldon or other sea salt crystals

SEL
235g unsalted butter, softened
25g Maldon or other sea salt crystals

Whisk the butter in a large bowl using an electric whisk for about 2 minutes until pale and mousse-like. Scrunch over the sea salt using your fingers, then work it into the butter using a wooden spoon until it is evenly distributed. Shape this into a patty or roll, or two, and wrap in waxed paper (baking paper is fine here).

DEMI-SEL
HIGH IN VIT A | SOURCE OF VITS D, E, IODINE
(per 10g serving) Energy 70 Kcal | Fat 7.7g | Sat fat 4.9g | Carbs 0g | Sugar 0g | Protein 0g | Salt 0.6g

SEL
HIGH IN VIT A | SOURCE OF VITS D, B12, IODINE
(per 10g serving) Energy 67 Kcal | Fat 7.4g | Sat fat 4.7g | Carbs 0g | Sugar 0g | Protein 0g | Salt 1g

Top left: Sweet bread spread with salted butter **Top right:** French *sel gris* and Maldon sea salt
Bottom left: Adding salt to whisked butter **Bottom right** Salted butter shaped into a roll

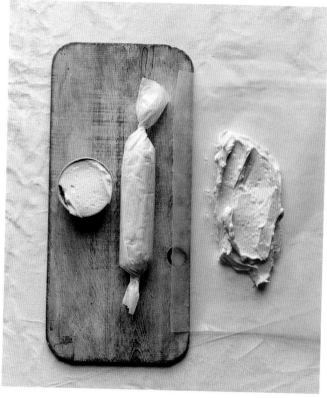

BOWL OF SOUP

WATERCRESS AND PISTACHIO SOUP WITH MISO BUTTER

There is a delightful small country house restaurant in Blainville-sur-Mer in Normandy called Le Mascaret, which is our special treat venue when we are after a little more than the spit and sawdust of the seaside cafés. Here they take aperitif offerings (in the form of rolls and butter) to new heights. A trolley laden with multiple mystery pots of aromatics ranging from honey to lavender, crushed nuts and spices, with baskets of warm bread and a wooden tub of freshly churned butter, is ceremoniously wheeled from table to table. First you chose your aromatics, and each in turn is pounded with a little butter using the back of a wooden paddle for spreading onto a warm roll. Miso butter was a winner, upbeat umami married to the rich creaminess of Normandy butter, a sophisticated Marmite finger.

Serves 6

1 tablespoon extra virgin olive oil
50g unsalted butter, softened
1 large onion, peeled and chopped
1 tablespoon finely chopped fresh ginger
100g shelled pistachio nuts
1 courgette, ends removed, halved lengthways and sliced
150ml white wine
750ml chicken stock
sea salt, black pepper
150g watercress, coarsely chopped
20g miso

Heat the olive oil with 10g of the butter in a large saucepan over a medium heat and fry the onion, ginger and pistachios for 5–7 minutes until the onion is starting to colour, stirring frequently. Add the courgette and fry for a few minutes longer until this too starts to colour and the nuts are toasty. Add the wine and simmer until well reduced. Add the stock and some seasoning, bring to the boil and simmer for 5 minutes, stirring in the watercress a minute before the end. Liquidise the soup in a blender in batches until as smooth as possible.

While the soup is cooking, work the remaining butter in a small bowl until it is really soft and creamy, then add the miso and blend to streak the butter. Serve the hot soup with a teaspoon of the butter melting in the middle.

HIGH IN VIT K
Energy 195 Kcal | Fat 14.7g | Sat fat 5.4g | Carbs 5.7g | Sugar 3.6g | Protein 4.7g | Salt 1.3g

SWEET POTATO AND CUMIN SOUP WITH FETA YOGURT

Sweet potatoes in a soup are promise of a thick, comforting and mealy bowlful. In fact, roasting aside, I think this has to be one of the best ways of eating them, pleasingly contrasted with some sharp feta. And it's the orange-fleshed potatoes you want here rather than the cream-coloured ones.

Serves 6

FOR THE SOUP
3 tablespoons extra virgin olive oil
1 large onion, peeled and chopped
4 garlic cloves, peeled and finely chopped
1 heaped teaspoon ground cumin
pinch of dried chilli flakes
1kg orange-fleshed sweet potatoes, peeled and thickly sliced
1.2 litres chicken or vegetable stock
sea salt

TO SERVE
75g feta, crumbled
150g low-fat Greek yogurt
2 tablespoons finely chopped sun-dried tomato (optional)

Heat the oil in a large saucepan over a medium heat, add the onion and fry for a few minutes until relaxed and glossy, stirring occasionally, then add the garlic, cumin and chilli flakes and fry for a further minute. Add the sweet potato, and continue to cook for another couple of minutes, stirring frequently. Pour in the stock and season with salt, bring to the boil and simmer over a low heat for 20 minutes, by which time the potato should be meltingly tender. Liquidise the soup in batches in a blender. Return it to the saucepan and season with a little more salt if necessary.

Combine the feta and yogurt in a bowl and serve spooned on top of the soup, each one scattered with a teaspoon of chopped sun-dried tomato if wished.

HIGH IN VIT A
Energy 304 Kcal | Fat 11.9g | Sat fat 3.2g | Carbs 39.7g | Sugar 13.4g | Protein 6.4g | Salt 1.5g

BROCCOLI AND CORIANDER SOUP WITH TAHINI

This sprightly tahini cream, at home lavished over any vegetable soup, provides that extra dimension, as do sun-dried tomatoes and coriander, which are deliciously aromatic.

Serves 4

FOR THE SOUP

2 tablespoons extra virgin olive oil
4 banana shallots, peeled, halved and sliced
1 scant teaspoon finely chopped medium–hot red chilli
3 garlic cloves, peeled and finely chopped
150ml white wine
approx. 500g small broccoli florets (2 heads)
sea salt
1 litre chicken stock
2 large handfuls of coriander, plus a little extra, coarsely chopped, to serve
2 tablespoons sun-dried tomato paste

FOR THE TAHINI CREAM

25g tahini paste
25g low-fat Greek yogurt
1 tablespoon lemon juice
1–3 tablespoons water

Heat the olive oil in a large saucepan over a medium heat and fry the shallots for 7–8 minutes until golden, stirring frequently and adding the chilli halfway through, and the garlic just before the end. Add the wine and simmer until well reduced. Add the broccoli, some salt and a little of the stock and cook for about 5 minutes, stirring frequently until it is well coated. Add the remaining stock, bring to the boil and simmer for 15 minutes or until the broccoli is tender.

Meanwhile, blend the tahini and yogurt in a small bowl, then work in the lemon juice and enough water to achieve a thick drizzling consistency, and season with a little salt. This can be made well in advance.*

Blitz the soup in a blender with the coriander and sun-dried tomato paste, and taste for seasoning. Serve the soup with a little of the tahini cream drizzled over, scattered with a little extra coriander.

*If making the tahini cream in advance, you may need to add a drop more water to loosen it.

HIGH IN VITS K, C
Energy 217 Kcal | Fat 13.9g | Sat fat 2g | Carbs 5.2g | Sugar 4.1g | Protein 8.7g | Salt 1.1g

Left: Celery, Apple and Gorgonzola Soup (page 62) **Middle:** Broccoli and Coriander Soup with Tahini **Right:** Carrot, Hazelnut and Thyme Soup (page 62)

LF CARROT, HAZELNUT AND THYME SOUP

Carrot soup, like banana cake or brownies, is one of those foods that we can return to again and again with fresh ideas or a new way of cooking it – you can't have too many recipes. The selling point here is the hazelnuts, which render it deliciously sweet and aromatic, and thick. It is a soup that shows just how good a humble little bowlful of buttery carrot can be.

Serves 4

700g carrots, trimmed, peeled and sliced
1 onion, peeled and chopped
125ml white wine
40g salted butter, diced, plus extra to serve
1 teaspoon sea salt
1 teaspoon caster sugar
a suspicion of cayenne pepper
50g hazelnuts, roasted and chopped
700ml chicken or vegetable stock
1 teaspoon soft thyme leaves, plus extra to serve

Place the carrots and onion in a medium saucepan with the wine, butter, salt, sugar and just a shake of cayenne pepper. Bring to the boil, then cover and simmer over a low heat for 8 minutes. Give the carrots a stir, turn the heat up to high and cook, uncovered, until all the wine has evaporated. Stir in the hazelnuts, add the stock, bring to the boil and simmer for 5 minutes, then purée the soup in a blender.

Return the soup to the saucepan and reheat if necessary, stir in the thyme leaves and serve with a few extra scattered over, with a small knob of butter in the centre of each bowl (see page 60).

HIGH IN VIT A
Energy 281 Kcal | Fat 17.3g | Sat fat 6.0g | Carbs 18.5g | Sugar 16.1g | Protein 4.2g | Salt 2.7g

LF CELERY, APPLE AND GORGONZOLA SOUP

This silky pale green soup is enlivened by the sharpness of the apple and the salty kick of a little Gorgonzola. One tip is to use only the very tender celery stalks to avoid having to sieve the soup – it is the leeks and apples that account for its nourishing texture.

Serves 4

15g unsalted butter
1 tablespoon rapeseed or extra virgin olive oil, plus extra for drizzling
3 leeks, trimmed and sliced
2 celery hearts (palest green tender stems and leaves only), trimmed and sliced
sea salt, black pepper
3 garlic cloves, peeled and finely chopped
2 eating apples, peeled, quartered, cored and diced
800ml chicken or vegetable stock
40g Gorgonzola piccante, finely crumbled, to serve

Melt the butter with the oil in a large saucepan over a medium heat, add the leeks and celery, season with salt and fry for 8–10 minutes until glossy and relaxed, stirring occasionally. Stir in the garlic and apple and continue to fry for a further 4–5 minutes until starting to colour. Add the stock, bring to the boil and simmer over a low heat for 15 minutes. Purée the soup in a blender with a grinding of black pepper.

Serve in warm bowls with a little Gorgonzola scattered over and a drizzle of oil (see page 60).

Energy 173 Kcal | Fat 10.4g | Sat fat 4.5g | Carbs 10.9g | Sugar 9.4g | Protein 5.5g | Salt 1.7g

CHILLED CUCUMBER, HAZELNUT AND YOGURT SOUP

Spain and Turkey meet in the centre of this bowl of chilled yogurt soup, which takes some ten minutes to whizz up. Just think of how many suppers where there are only two of you when this soup might tick the box, especially come those fine summer evenings when it gets harder and harder to drag yourself away from the idyll of the garden early evening.

Though in common with many gazpachos that include ground nuts, it also benefits from being being chilled for a couple of hours to allow the nuts to soften and thicken the soup, just slightly. So even better, you can whizz it up at teatime and have the whole of the evening to bliss out. You can also make this using 0%-fat Greek yogurt.

Serves 2

30g hazelnuts
1 cucumber, ends removed, peeled and cut up
handful of mint leaves, plus a little extra, finely chopped, to serve
handful of flat-leaf parsley leaves
1 garlic clove, peeled and chopped
1 teaspoon finely chopped medium–hot red chilli
2 slim spring onions, trimmed and sliced
200g natural Greek yogurt, plus extra to serve
2 tablespoons extra virgin olive oil
1 tablespoon lemon juice
1 level teaspoon caster sugar
sea salt
pomegranate syrup, to serve

Grind the nuts as finely as possible in an electric coffee grinder. Transfer them to a blender, add all the remaining ingredients and whizz until smooth. It will be delicious eaten straight away if you are in a hurry, but otherwise pour it into a bowl or jug, cover and chill for a couple of hours. It will still be delicious the following day.

Serve with a spoon of yogurt, a little chopped mint and a drizzle of pomegranate syrup.

HIGH IN VIT K | SOURCE OF VITS E, C, MANGANESE
Energy 291 Kcal | Fat 21.9g | Sat fat 2.9g | Carbs 13.1g | Sugar 11.8g | Protein 9g | Salt 0.2g

LF CAULIFLOWER SOUP WITH HALLOUMI CROUTONS

Even better than bread croutons, toasty little nibs of halloumi. This cheese exists to be fried, and in the company of cauliflower has something of the timeless allure of cauliflower cheese. And how good it is to see that chard, which also stars, has finally become a regular green on the shelves, especially when it is young and rainbow.

Serves 6

FOR THE SOUP
25g unsalted butter
1 onion, peeled, halved and sliced
3 garlic cloves, peeled and finely chopped
approx. 700g small cauliflower florets (1 medium head)
large handful of flat-leaf parsley
1 tablespoon crème fraîche
sea salt
freshly grated nutmeg

FOR THE CHARD AND HALLOUMI
1½ tablespoons extra virgin olive oil
200g young chard*, stalks sliced 1cm thick, leaves coarsely chopped
100g halloumi, cut into 1cm dice
squeeze of lemon juice

Melt the butter in a large saucepan over a medium heat, add the onion, garlic and cauliflower and stir to coat them, then add 100ml of the water and cook for 8–10 minutes until this evaporates, without the veg colouring, stirring occasionally. Add 900ml of water, bring to the boil, cover and cook over a low heat for 25 minutes.

Purée the soup in a blender with the parsley, crème fraîche and a little salt and nutmeg until silky and flecked with green.

Heat a tablespoon of oil in a large non-stick frying pan over a medium heat, add the chard stalks and fry for a couple of minutes until beginning to colour, stirring frequently, and then add half the leaves. Once these have wilted, add the remainder and continue to fry for a couple of minutes until wilted and tender. Transfer this to a bowl, add the remaining oil to the pan and fry the halloumi for several minutes until golden and toasted, stirring frequently. Squeeze over a little lemon juice.

If necessary, reheat the soup and serve with a spoonful of the chard in the centre of each bowl and some of the halloumi croutons scattered over.

*You need skinny chard stalks here, 1–1.5cm thick, and if you have the choice of rainbow, so much the prettier.

SOURCE OF VITS K, C, FOLATE
Energy 188 Kcal | Fat 12.7g | Sat fat 6.5g | Carbs 7g | Sugar 4.8g | Protein 9.5g | Salt 0.3g

ROAST SQUASH, CHILLI AND CORIANDER SOUP

This roast vegetable soup that is full of South American pizzazz would be nowhere without its finishing flourish of soured cream. As punchy as it is simple, there is no careful stirring or frying, instead the caramelisation takes place in the oven and the flavours concentrate in the process.

Serves 6

FOR THE SOUP

1.5–1.6kg butternut squash, skin and seeds discarded, and cut into chunks
2 large onions, peeled, halved and sliced
4 vine tomatoes, halved
1 medium–hot red chilli (5–7cm long)
4 tablespoons extra virgin olive oil
sea salt
900ml chicken or vegetable stock

TO SERVE

2 tablespoons soured cream
coarsely chopped coriander
pickled piri-piri or jalapeño peppers (optional)

Preheat the oven to 200°C fan/220°C/gas mark 6. Arrange the squash, onions and tomatoes in a couple of large roasting pans so that they fit in a crowded single layer, adding the chilli to one. Drizzle a couple of tablespoons of oil over each roasting pan and season with salt. Roast for 55 minutes, stirring halfway through.

Remove from the oven, and if any of the onion strands are particularly dark, discard these. Scrape out the inside of the chilli, discarding the seeds if possible, and liquidise the vegetables with the stock in batches in a blender. Pass through a sieve into a saucepan.

Gently reheat and serve with a spoon of soured cream, some chopped coriander and pickled chilli if wished.

HIGH IN VIT A | SOURCE OF VIT C
Energy 248 Kcal | Fat 11.2g | Sat fat 3g | Carbs 28.2g | Sugar 17.3g | Protein 4.9g | Salt 0.8g

MASALA LENTIL SOUP WITH CUCUMBER RAITA

A cucumber raita is a good call in a lentil soup, a reckoning of textures. Garam masala is a soup's answer to curry, the best blends being elegant and balanced, with a touch of heat but without the full-on blast of most curry powders. This makes a generous quantity, but lentil soup is the stuff of main courses, and this allows you to return for more.

Serves 8

FOR THE SOUP
4 tablespoons groundnut or vegetable oil
2 leeks, trimmed and sliced
4 carrots, trimmed, peeled and sliced
1 celery heart, trimmed and sliced
1 heaped teaspoon garam masala
4 garlic cloves, peeled and finely chopped
500g red lentils, rinsed
3 tablespoons lemon or lime juice
2 litres chicken or vegetable stock
sea salt

FOR THE CUCUMBER RAITA
½ cucumber, ends discarded, peeled, quartered and finely sliced
125g natural Greek yogurt
large pinch of caster sugar
ground cumin for dusting

Heat the oil in a large saucepan over a medium heat, add the leeks, carrots and celery and fry for about 10 minutes until softened and starting to colour, stirring frequently, then add the garam masala and garlic and cook for a few minutes longer. Stir in the lentils, add the lemon or lime juice, then pour in the stock and season with salt.

Bring to the boil, skim off any surface foam and simmer for 30 minutes or until the lentils are tender. Purée in batches in a blender, then taste for seasoning.

While the soup is cooking, place the cucumber in a bowl, toss with a liberal sprinkling of salt and set aside for 30 minutes to draw out the juices. Rinse the cucumber in a sieve and pat dry on kitchen paper.

Blend the yogurt with the sugar and a little salt in a bowl, then fold in the cucumber. Serve the raita dolloped in the centre of the soup, dusted with cumin.

SOURCE OF VIT A
Energy 310 Kcal | Fat 8.4g | Sat fat 2.3g | Carbs 38.5g | Sugar 5.5g | Protein 17g | Salt 0.7g

MUSHROOM SOUP WITH SPELT, PESTO AND YOGURT

A spoonful of freshly cooked spelt grains stirred into this soup at the end is the idealised take, but any grain will do and the pouches of ready-cooked quinoa and the like are a game-changer. I don't go in for much in the way of convenience, but every now and again something brilliant presents itself, and such brown rice, lentils and whole grains are one of the best things to hit the shelves recently. They're also ideal when you only want a small amount.

Serves 6

FOR THE SOUP
15g dried porcini
150ml boiling water
2 tablespoons extra virgin olive oil
25g unsalted butter
1 onion, peeled and chopped
3 garlic cloves, peeled and finely chopped
700g button mushrooms, stalks trimmed and sliced
sea salt, black pepper
100ml medium sherry
800ml chicken stock
6 tablespoons cooked spelt

TO SERVE
1 heaped tablespoon pesto
2 tablespoons natural Greek yogurt

Cover the dried mushrooms with the boiling water in a small bowl and leave to soak for 15 minutes. Heat the olive oil and butter in a large saucepan over a medium heat and fry the onion for about 5 minutes until softened and glossy, stirring frequently, adding the garlic just before the end. Add the mushrooms, season generously with salt and a little pepper and fry for about 5 minutes longer until they are soft and have given out their juices, again stirring occasionally. Add the sherry and simmer to reduce the liquid by half.

Slice the soaked mushrooms and add these and the liquor to the pan, along with the stock. Bring to the boil, cover and cook over a low heat for 15 minutes. Purée the soup in batches in a blender, return it to a clean pan, stir in the spelt and gently reheat. Serve dotted with pesto and a dollop of yogurt.

Energy 201 Kcal | Fat 10.9g | Sat fat 3.9g | Carbs 11.2g | Sugar 3.9g | Protein 8.3g | Salt 0.8g

BUTTERED BEETROOT SOUP WITH DILL

The colour of this soup is readily imagined as the setting sun over a sea's horizon; only the most cynical could fail to have their mood lifted at the sight of a pan of this on the hob. Sweet and fragrant as well as wholesome, for which we have butter to thank, as it infuses the vegetables before they are simmered, and affords the soup its inimitable body. The crème fraîche is optional, but an added thrill of a creamy ivory river bleeding into the rich vermilion.

Serves 6

FOR THE SOUP
600g large carrots, trimmed, peeled and thickly sliced
600g beetroot, trimmed, peeled, quartered and thickly sliced
2 banana shallots, peeled, halved and sliced
200ml medium–dry cider
50g unsalted butter, diced
sea salt, black pepper
1 litre chicken or vegetable stock

TO SERVE
2 tablespoons crème fraîche
snipped dill

Put the carrots and beetroot in a large saucepan with the shallots, cider, butter and some salt. Give everything a stir, bring the liquid to a simmer, then cover and cook over a medium heat for 8 minutes. Stir the vegetables, turn the heat up and cook, uncovered, for 8–12 minutes until all the liquid evaporates and they are glossy and coated in a buttery emulsion, stirring towards the end. Add the stock and bring to the boil, then simmer for 15 minutes or until the vegetables are meltingly tender.

Liquidise the soup in batches in a blender. Serve with a spoon of crème fraîche in the centre, scattered with dill and with a grinding of black pepper.

HIGH IN VIT A | SOURCE OF FOLATE
Energy 220 Kcal | Fat 13.5g | Sat fat 8.5g | Carbs 16.4g | Sugar 15.1g | Protein 3.1g | Salt 1.1g

SOMETHING LIGHT: DIPS, EATS & MELTS

WALNUT AND RYE SODA BREAD

A wholemeal walnut loaf has to be one of the finest crumbs for serving with cheese, and not something that we can readily buy, so this easy recipe is a real boon to have up your sleeve.

The most elementary of breads, soda bread relies on bicarb and buttermilk for its rise, and has that alluring sour tint that is so good in a loaf. And for those shy of yeast cookery, you can knock this one up in ten minutes, as there's no proving involved – like American muffins, the art lies in slapdash mixing. Delicious eaten newly cooled or slightly warm with some farmhouse cheddar and chutney, in addition to all the following dips and pâtés.

Makes 1 × 600g loaf

unsalted butter for greasing the tin
120g wholemeal rye flour, plus extra for kneading and flouring the tin
120g plain flour
60g walnuts, coarsely chopped
¾ teaspoon sea salt
¾ teaspoon bicarbonate of soda, sifted
1 medium free-range egg
284ml buttermilk

Preheat the oven to 190°C fan/210°C/gas mark 6½. Butter a 22cm/1.1-litre non-stick loaf tin and dust with wholemeal flour. Combine the flours, nuts, salt and bicarbonate of soda in a large bowl. Whisk the egg and buttermilk together in a medium bowl, tip onto the dry ingredients and mix with a wooden spoon until roughly blended, then bring the dough together using your hands. It will be sticky at this point, so throw another handful of flour over and turn it over a couple of times to smooth it a little, without kneading.

Gently press the dough into the tin, and mark a line down the centre about 1cm deep. Dust with a little wholemeal flour and bake for 30–35 minutes until risen and golden. Run a knife around the edge and tip the loaf out of the tin – the base should sound hollow when tapped. Leave it to cool on a wire rack. It will be good for several days eaten cold. The bread can also be reheated: wrap in foil and put in the oven for 15 minutes at 160°C fan /180°C/ gas mark 4.

SOURCE OF VITS D, B1, FIBRE, FOLATE, PHOSPHOROUS, MANGANESE
(per 25g serving) Energy 60 Kcal | Fat 2.2g | Sat fat 0.4g | Carbs 7.6g | Sugar 0.7g | Protein 1.9g | Salt 0.2g

LF CROUTONS

For any of the dips and the like that follow.

Makes 18/Serves 6

approx. ½ small, day-old French baton
extra virgin olive oil, for brushing

Preheat the oven to 180°C fan/200°C/gas mark 6. Slice the French baton into 18 croutons about 5mm thick. Lay these out on a baking sheet and bake for 5 minutes to dry them out. Brush with olive oil either side and return to the oven for 10–12 minutes until golden – you may need to remove them gradually as they are ready. Leave to cool on a wire rack. They can be made a day in advance, in which case store them in an airtight container.

SOURCE OF VIT B1, FIBRE, MANGANESE
Energy 109 Kcal | Fat 2.5g | Sat fat 0.4g | Carbs 17.8g | Sugar 0.9g | Protein 3.3g | Salt 0.5g

DIPS

SMOKED SALMON, LEMON AND QUARK PÂTÉ

One to challenge that bought tub, providing lots of protein power, with the added bonus of a dose of omega 3 as well as calcium. It has a luxurious silky texture without being too rich, so you can scoop it onto slivers of cucumber and toast with some abandon.

Serves 6

FOR THE PÂTÉ
150g smoked salmon, brown meat cut out
½ teaspoon finely grated lemon zest, plus 1 tablespoon juice
150g quark (for homemade see page 46)
1 heaped tablespoon soured cream
couple of shakes of Tabasco
black pepper

TO TOP
2 heaped tablespoons finely chopped chives

Whizz all the ingredients for the pâté in a food processor until smooth and creamy, then spoon into a shallow bowl (approx. 12cm) and smooth the surface. Liberally sprinkle the surface with the chives, and gently press these into the pâté. Cover and chill until required.

HIGH IN VIT B12 | SOURCE OF VITS B2, B3, PHOSPHOROUS, SELENIUM
Energy 62 Kcal | Fat 1.8g | Sat fat 0.6g | Carbs 1.2g | Sugar 1.2g | Protein 10.2g | Salt 1.2g

SMOKED MACKEREL AND HORSERADISH PÂTÉ

Smoked mackerel with horseradish is a hard marriage to beat that aspires to the sort of savouries that fuelled gentlemen's clubs of old. The fish is rich in its own right, so it only calls for the minimum of butter, together with some quark that is altogether leaner than cream cheese. Hard to have too many batons of carrot for dipping, in addition to the radishes, and quail eggs too.

Serves 6

FOR THE PÂTÉ
30g unsalted butter, softened
100g quark
2 teaspoons horseradish sauce
200g smoked mackerel fillets, skinned
2 teaspoons lemon juice
black pepper

TO TOP
1 tablespoon small capers, e.g. nonpareille, rinsed and dried on kitchen paper
cayenne pepper, for dusting

Whizz the butter in a food processor until really creamy, then add the quark and horseradish and continue to whizz until well-blended. Add the mackerel and whizz to a coarse pate, then add the lemon juice and season with black pepper.

HIGH IN VITS D, B3, B12, SELENIUM, IODINE | SOURCE OF VITS A, B2, B6, PHOSPHOROUS
Energy 172 Kcal | Fat 14.6g | Sat fat 4.7g | Carbs 1.2g | Sugar 0.9g | Protein 8.9g | Salt 0.9g

Top left: Café-style Chicken Liver and Port Pâté Top right: Smoked Salmon, Lemon and Quark Pâté (page 75) Bottom left: Smoked Mackerel and Horseradish Pâté (page 75) Bottom right Walnut and Rye Soda Bread (page 74)

CAFÉ-STYLE CHICKEN LIVER AND PORT PÂTÉ

There is every reason to make your own pâté; as a peruse of the back of the pack of bought types will reveal that they may contain up to three-quarters pork fat despite being advertised as duck or rabbit. That said, even a homemade chicken liver pâté can run to indecent amounts of butter, when more isn't necessarily tastier. By upping the chicken livers, which play the lead role, this is gutsier than many, and altogether more rustic.

Poaching the chicken livers instead of frying them was an inspired tip given to me by an inspired artist, the aunt of a friend I have known since school who is one of the best cooks I have ever met. Oenone Acheson says her daughters beg her to make chicken liver pâté every time they visit from Spain. Poaching them avoids the usual hazard of the chicken livers spitting hot oil when you fry them.

Serves 6

FOR THE PÂTÉ
400g free-range chicken livers, fatty membranes removed
75g unsalted butter, softened and diced
1 banana shallot, peeled and finely chopped
1 garlic clove, peeled and finely chopped
1 heaped tablespoon soft thyme leaves
3 tablespoons port
1 tablespoon soured cream
sea salt, black pepper
freshly grated nutmeg

TO TOP
a few bay leaves
pink or green peppercorns

Bring a medium pan of water to the boil, add the chicken livers and poach for 2 minutes, then drain into a sieve. Melt a knob of the butter in a large frying pan over a medium heat and fry the shallot and garlic with the thyme for a minute or two until glossy and translucent. Add the port and simmer until well reduced and syrupy, then stir in the chicken livers.

Purée the contents of the frying pan in a food processor with the soured cream and plenty of salt, pepper and nutmeg. Leave this to cool for about 20 minutes, then incorporate the remaining butter. Press through a sieve into a large bowl.

Spoon the pâté into a shallow bowl (approx. 12cm), smooth the surface and top with the bay leaves and peppercorns. Cover and chill.

HIGH IN VITS A, B1, B2, B3, B5, B6, B7, B12, FOLATE, IRON | SOURCE OF VIT C, PHOSPHOROUS, ZINC, MANGANESE Energy 177 Kcal | Fat 12.6g | Sat fat 7.5g | Carbs 1.6g | Sugar 1.1g | Protein 12.2g | Salt 0.3g

AMERICAN BLUE CHEESE DIP

This is the dip that smothered the salad that came with the barbecue ribs that had you going back for another leaf or two. No denying it is on the rich side, but with such presence courtesy of the king of the blues – Roquefort – a little goes a long way. Delectable whether you have a small bowl to the side of some courgette chips, dished up with some crudités (slivers of celery heart are especially good) or turned into a salad with crispy lardons.

Serves 4

50g soured cream
30g mayonnaise
1 teaspoon lemon juice
couple of shakes of Tabasco
75g Roquefort, finely crumbled, plus a little extra to serve
2 tablespoons natural yogurt
1 tablespoon finely chopped chives, plus a few extra to serve

Blend the soured cream, mayonnaise, lemon juice and Tabasco in a small bowl. Gently mash the Roquefort and yogurt in another small bowl, simply to acquaint the two and soften the cheese around the edges, but without reducing it to a purée. Fold this into the dressing base, then the chives. Transfer to a small serving bowl, and scatter a little extra cheese and some chives over the top. Cover and chill. It will keep well for several days.

HIGH IN CALCIUM | SOURCE OF VITS A, D, B2, PHOSPHOROUS
Energy 171 Kcal | Fat 15.8g | Sat fat 6.8g | Carbs 2g | Sugar 2g | Protein 5.4g | Salt 0.9g

LF AVOCADO, CORIANDER AND LIME DIP

This makes a change from guacamole, but has the same charm. Serve it as a dip with shell-on prawns and breadsticks, or as an accompaniment to grilled chicken and lamb chops, as well as dolloping it onto quesadillas (see page 101).

Serves 6

flesh of 2 avocados
1 tablespoon lime juice
1 large handful coriander, plus extra to serve
couple of shakes of Tabasco
sea salt
pinch of caster sugar
1 heaped tablespoon soured cream
1 tablespoon extra virgin olive oil, plus extra to serve

Whizz all the ingredients in a food processor until smooth and creamy. Transfer to a shallow bowl (approx. 12cm) smoothing the surface, cover and chill until required. Drizzle over a little oil and scatter with coriander just before serving. It will keep well for a day.

SOURCE OF VITS E, C, B6, FIBRE, POTASSIUM
Energy 92 Kcal | Fat 9.1g | Sat fat 2.2g | Carbs 1.2g | Sugar 0.7g | Protein 0.7g | Salt trace

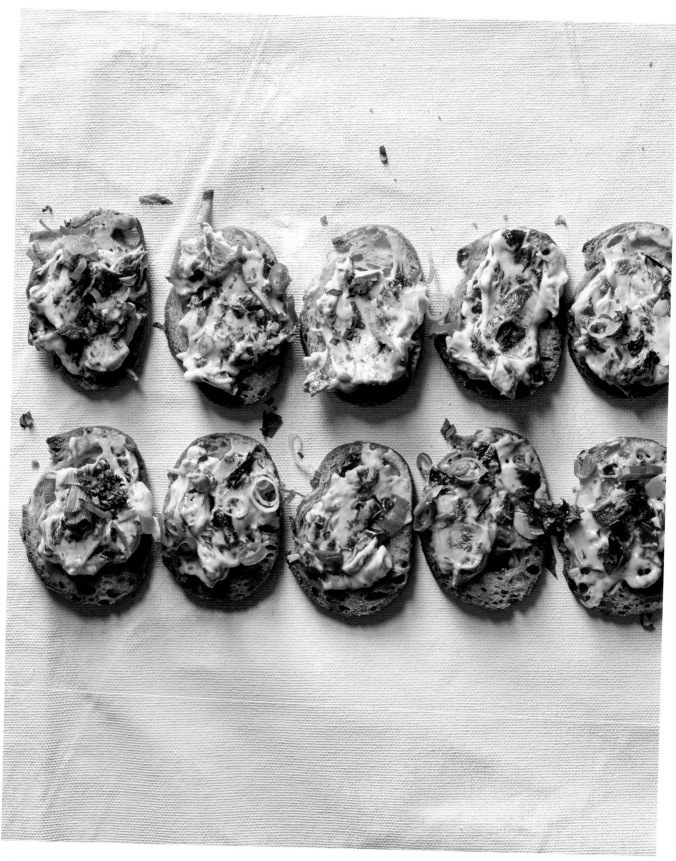

ROASTED RED PEPPER, GOAT'S CHEESE AND MINT DIP

Shades of Morroco here, which makes it an adept summer standby to have in the fridge when friends drop in unexpectedly, for dipping and slathering onto croutons with a small glass of something.

Serves 6

3 red, yellow or orange peppers
2 tablespoons extra virgin olive oil, plus extra to serve
sea salt, black pepper
150g young goat's cheese
75g low-fat fromage frais
squeeze of lemon juice
2 heaped teaspoons finely chopped spring onion
1 heaped tablespoon finely chopped mint
cayenne pepper, for dusting

Preheat the oven to 190°C/fan/210°C/gas mark 6½. Cut out the core from each pepper, then quarter them, discarding any seeds inside, and arrange in a crowded single layer in a roasting pan. Drizzle over the oil and season with salt and pepper.

Roast for about 50 minutes, stirring every 20 minutes to ensure that the peppers emerge succulent and evenly singed at the edges. Leave to cool.

Chop the peppers into approx. 1cm dice. Whizz the goat's cheese and fromage frais in a food processor until smooth, then add a squeeze of lemon. Transfer to a medium bowl and stir in the diced peppers, the spring onion and the mint. Spoon into small serving bowls, drizzle over a little oil and dust with cayenne pepper.

HIGH IN VITS A, C | SOURCE OF VITS D, B6
Energy 147 Kcal | Fat 10.5g | Sat fat 5.1g | Carbs 5.2g | Sugar 4.8g | Protein 7.1g | Salt 0.4g

GREEN GODDESS RICOTTA

These kinds of dip-intos are a mainstay of my fridge, to serve with leftover roast veggies, asparagus and long-stem broccoli spears, as well as crudités, green olives and pickled green chillies.

Serves 4

50g mint and basil leaves, plus a few extra small leaves
3 slim spring onions, trimmed and coarsely sliced
1 small or ½ garlic clove, peeled and chopped
2 tablespoons extra virgin olive oil, plus extra to serve
sea salt
250g ricotta, drained
1 tablespoon lemon juice

Whizz the herbs, spring onions and garlic with the olive oil and a little salt to a paste in a food processor, then add the ricotta and whizz again, and finally add the lemon juice. Transfer this to a serving bowl, cover and chill.

To serve, drizzle over a little more oil and scatter with a few small herb leaves.

SOURCE OF VIT A, CALCIUM, PHOSPHORUS
Energy 148 Kcal | Fat 12.5g | Sat fat 5.1g | Carbs 2.3g | Sugar 1.5g | Protein 6.5g | Salt 0.2g

GOAT'S CHEESE APPETISER

Marinated goat's cheese takes planning, and this comes laced with the same kind of aromatics, but can be whizzed up as a last-minute thought. It would look most at home on a big tray with some Parma ham, or even smoked salmon, a big rocket salad and toasted sourdough bread as a relaxed lunch. Very good with roast veg too.

Serves 6

300g young or semi-mature goat's cheese
2 heaped tablespoons finely chopped flat-leaf parsley
finely grated zest of 1 lemon
1 garlic clove, peeled and finely chopped
6 tablespoons extra virgin olive oil

Crumble the goat's cheese into 1–2cm pieces and scatter over the base of a shallow dish. Combine the parsley, lemon zest and garlic in a medium bowl and scatter over the goat's cheese, then drizzle over the oil. Cover and chill. It keeps well for several days.

HIGH IN VITS A, K | SOURCE OF VITS C, B2, B12, PHOSPHOROUS, IODINE
Energy 261 Kcal | Fat 24g | Sat fat 10.5g | Carbs 0.7g | Sugar 0.6g | Protein 10.5g | Salt 0.8g

TOUCH OF BOURSIN

Much as we love Boursin, it comes in at a hefty 40% fat, so while this is a pretender to the throne, it does boast a fraction of that. But the flavours are all there and the creamy texture too.

Chervil is a shy little leaf that we don't see nearly enough of, but should it present itself, use a teaspoonful in lieu of the parsley for a French accent. Also, to make life easy, you might like to use a spreadable butter instead of softening up a block. If you make this using your own fromage frais (see page 46), then you have the satisfaction of a really homespun cream cheese.

Serves 4

300g low-fat fromage frais (to yield approx. 200g strained fromage frais, see method)
25g unsalted butter, softened
1 small garlic clove, peeled and crushed to a paste
2 teaspoons finely chopped chives
2 teaspoons finely chopped flat-leaf parsley
fine sea salt
coarsely ground black pepper or paprika, to serve

Place a sieve over a bowl the same diameter. Line the sieve with a double thickness of kitchen paper, tip the fromage frais into it, loosely cover with clingfilm and chill overnight to drain off the whey.

Carefully tip the strained fromage frais into a medium bowl, peeling off the wet paper. Add the butter and blend using a wooden spoon, then blend in the remaining ingredients. Transfer this to a small serving dish and either scatter over a little coarsely crushed black pepper if you want to keep it in Boursin mode, or a little paprika. Cover and chill until required. It should keep well for several days.

SOURCE OF VITS A, K, B2, B12, CALCIUM, PHOSPHOROUS, IODINE
Energy 15 Kcal | Fat 0.9g | Sat fat 0.6g | Carbs 0.7g | Sugar 0.6g | Protein 1g | Salt trace

EATS

RETRO EATS

Sometimes it is the slightly dated titbits that get hoovered up over a drink or two, and both these tick the box. I think it is because everyone has memories of a snack of this nature at some family do as a child, so they have that sense of comfort and safeness. Manchego and pickled chilli (nothing wrong in that) are brilliant with honey, and jars of Peppadew peppers are a sneak cheat to have handy.

Serves 4

CHEESE 'N' CHILLI EATS

Arrange about 16 slim wedges (120g–150g) of Manchego or pecorino sardo on a couple of plates, and lay a small pickled chilli (or half a long one), e.g. Fragata guindillas, on top. You can do this well in advance. Drizzle over 1–2 tablespoons of runny honey to serve.

HIGH IN VITS A, B12, CALCIUM, PHOSPHOROUS | SOURCE OF VIT B2, ZINC
Energy 148 Kcal | Fat 11.2g | Sat fat 6.2g | Carbs 3.6g | Sugar 3.1g | Protein 8.2g | Salt 1g

Serves 4

PARTY PEPPADEWS

Stuff 120g hot Peppadew peppers with 120g young goat's curd (a table knife is easiest for this), dust with cayenne pepper and arrange on a bed of mustard and cress, or pile in a bowl.

HIGH IN VITS A, C | SOURCE OF PHOSPHOROUS
Energy 111 Kcal | Fat 8g | Sat fat 5.4g | Carbs 2.7g | Sugar 2.4g | Protein 6.7g | Salt 0.5g

LF RAREBIT BLINIS WITH PICCALILLI

An entente cordiale between Russia and the UK, tender little blinis smothered with rarebit.

Makes 16/Serves 6

FOR THE RAREBIT MIXTURE
20g day-old white bread (excluding crusts)
120g Red Leicester, cut into chunks
15g unsalted butter
2 tablespoons stout
½ teaspoon Dijon mustard
1 teaspoon Worcestershire sauce
1 medium free-range egg white

FOR THE BLINIS
16 cocktail blinis
piccalilli, to serve

Whizz the bread to crumbs in a food processor. Add all the remaining ingredients for the mixture and blend to a paste. Thickly spread the blinis with the rarebit mixture. You can make these up well in advance, in which case cover and chill.

You need to grill them under a lowish grill to cook the inside of the mixture, either under a medium heat for 5–7 minutes or under a low heat for about 5 minutes, turning it up to brown the top. Either way, warm the baking sheet under the grill for 5–10 minutes in advance, to help crisp the base of the rarebits. Spoon about ¼ teaspoon piccalilli in the centre of each one. Serve straight away.

HIGH IN VITS A, B12, CALCIUM, PHOSPHOROUS | SOURCE OF VIT B2, ZINC, IODINE
Energy 42 Kcal | Fat 3.3g | Sat fat 2.1g | Carbs 0.7g | Sugar 0.2g | Protein 2.1g | Salt 0.2g

ASPARAGUS CIGARILLOS

A cult collection of goodies, neatly wrapped into parcels. Parma ham turns super crispy in the oven, and feta soft and mousse-like. These are a treat on their own if it's just the two of you; otherwise dive in there with some warmed flatbread, a tomato salad close at hand.

Serves 4

300g finger-thick asparagus (trimmed weight)
3 tablespoons extra virgin olive oil
sea salt, black pepper
8 slices Parma or other air-dried ham
125g feta, cut across into thin strips about 8cm long
1 large slice coarse-textured day-old white bread, crusts removed
2 teaspoons thyme leaves

Bring a large pan of salted water to the boil, add the asparagus and simmer for 3 minutes, then drain it into a colander, pass under the cold tap and leave to cool. Toss with a tablespoon of the oil and some seasoning.

Preheat the oven to 200°C fan/220°C/gas mark 7. Lay 2–3 asparagus spears across one end of each slice of ham with their tips protruding above the fat. Lay a slice of feta on top within the ham, then roll up into a parcel and arrange in a row in a roasting pan, feta upwards.

Whizz the bread to coarse crumbs or nibs in a food processor, and toss in a bowl with a tablespoon of oil and the thyme. Scatter over and around the parcels. (You can prepare them to this point well in advance, in which case cover and chill.)

Drizzle over a little more oil and bake for 15–20 minutes until the crumbs are golden.

HIGH IN FOLATE
Energy 264 Kcal | Fat 17.6g | Sat fat 6.9g | Carbs 6.5g | Sugar 2.1g | Protein 18.9g | Salt 3.3g

SPANISH OMELETTE WITH SOURED CREAM AND CHIVES

An easy take on a Spanish omelette with crispy sheathes of ham on top, delicious eaten hot with the soured cream and chive sauce, or warm with the sauce and a pile of green leaves, such as lightly dressed peashoots and mint, on top.

Serves 4

FOR THE OMELETTE
4 tablespoons extra virgin olive oil
1 onion, peeled, halved and thinly sliced
500g medium-sized waxy potatoes, peeled or scrubbed as necessary,
   and thickly sliced
sea salt, black pepper
6 medium free-range eggs
about 4 slices Parma or other air-dried ham

FOR THE SOURED CREAM AND CHIVE SAUCE
2 tablespoons finely chopped chives, plus extra to serve
150g soured cream

Heat 2 tablespoons of the olive oil in a 24cm non-stick frying pan with a heatproof handle over a medium heat, add the onion and fry for 5–6 minutes until lightly golden, stirring frequently. Add the potatoes and cook for another few minutes, turning them now and again, until they are coated in the oil. Season with salt, add 100ml of water to the pan, cover it with a large saucepan lid and cook over a low heat for about 10 minutes until the potatoes are just tender. Using the lid, drain off any excess water and leave, covered, to cool for about 15 minutes.

Whisk the eggs in a large bowl with a little seasoning, then stir in the potatoes and onion. Heat the grill to high, and also wipe out and reheat the pan over a medium heat. Add a tablespoon of oil to the pan, tip in the egg and potato mixture and cook for 3 minutes. Arrange the ham on top, leaving a rim of a couple of centimetres, drizzle over another tablespoon of oil and place under the grill for a few minutes until golden and puffy at the sides – it should be slightly moist in the centre.

Remove from the grill and leave the omelette to stand for 10 minutes, when it will continue to cook in the centre. Stir the chives into the soured cream, and season with salt. Serve this spooned on top of the hot or warm omelette with extra chives scattered over.

SOURCE OF VITS B6, B12
Energy 416 Kcal | Fat 27.4g | Sat fat 8.8g | Carbs 24.7g | Sugar 4.2g | Protein 15.9g | Salt 1g

LF FIG, GORGONZOLA AND BASIL CROUTES

A soigné hand-me-round or a relaxed stand-in for a starter at a barbecue or summer supper. The honey accentuates the sweetness of the figs as well as helping the caramelisation.

Serves 6

12 × 1cm-thick slices of baguette, lightly toasted
180g Gorgonzola, cut into 12 thick slices
3 figs (approx. 150g), stalks trimmed
extra virgin olive oil, for drizzling
3 tablespoons runny honey
a few tiny basil leaves, e.g. Greek, cut into thin strips

Preheat the grill to high. Spread each croute with a slice of Gorgonzola, taking it just within the rim. Cut a small slice off each fig either side, and then cut downwards into four slices. Lay a slice on each croute, and arrange in a roasting pan. Drizzle over a little olive oil and the honey and grill until the toast surround is nice and golden and the cheese is softened, without melting to a river. Scatter over the basil, then leave to cool for about 5 minutes before serving.

SOURCE OF VIT B2, CALCIUM, PHOSPHOROUS
Energy 249 Kcal | Fat 12.4g | Sat fat 6.6g | Carbs 24.6g | Sugar 9.2g | Protein 9.2g | Salt 1.7g

LF BURRATA WITH FIGS

As cheese with fruit goes, it is hard to concieve of a more luxurious take than a ball of burrata torn into soft creamy skeins with figs so ripe they are on their way to being jam. It's anything you want it to be from a light lunch with Parma ham to an indulgent end to supper.

Serves 4

200g burrata, torn into pieces
1 tablespoon extra virgin olive oil
1 tablespoon lemon juice
4 very ripe figs, stalks trimmed, halved downwards
sea salt

Arrange the torn burrata on a plate. Drizzle over the oil and lemon juice, then scatter over the fig halves and scrunch over a smidgeon of sea salt.

SOURCE OF VITS A, B2, B12, CALCIUM, PHOSPHOROUS, ZINC
Energy 170 Kcal | Fat 13.0g | Sat fat 7.3g | Carbs 3.2g | Sugar 3.2g | Protein 9.6g | Salt 0.5g

LF **HALLOUMI BURGERS WITH LEMON AND MINT**

MELTS

Halloumi toasts up beautifully with crispy golden edges and a gooey inside that holds its shape. It is, however, a salty cheese, so these burgers are designed to play on its strengths, while adding in a touch of sweet-sourness to balance out its saline character. And they're dead easy, mid-week supper material.

Serves 4

FOR THE BURGERS
200g halloumi, drained and coarsely grated
2 spring onions, trimmed, halved lengthways and finely sliced
2 handfuls coarsely chopped flat-leaf parsley
2 tablespoons finely chopped mint
finely grated zest of 1 lemon, plus a squeeze of juice
200g courgette, coarsely grated
1 medium free-range egg, beaten
4 teaspoons extra virgin olive oil

TO SERVE
150g cherry tomatoes, halved
sea salt
1 heaped teaspoon finely sliced medium–hot red chilli
6 warm small round pittas, slit
diced avocado or balsamic onion relish

Combine the halloumi, spring onions, herbs and lemon zest in a large bowl. You can do this well in advance, then cover and chill.

Shortly before serving, sprinkle the tomatoes with salt and set aside for 15–30 minutes, then stir in the chilli.

Add the courgette to the cheese mixture and mix well, then season with a little lemon juice and add the egg. Using an 8cm plain biscuit cutter or ring, press 3 heaped tablespoons of the mixture at a time into the ring to make small burgers 2–3cm thick – you should get six in all.

Heat 2 teaspoons of oil in a large non-stick frying pan over a medium–low heat and fry half the burgers at a time for 4–6 minutes on one side and about 3 minutes on the other side until golden and crusty, carefully lifting them with a spatula now and again to check, as they can darken quite quickly and they are quite delicate. Transfer these to a plate and keep warm in a low oven while you cook the remainder, adding the remaining oil to the pan.

Slip the burgers inside the pittas, add some diced avo or spread with some onion relish, and then scatter over the tomatoes.

Energy 563 Kcal | Fat 21.1g | Sat fat 9.8g | Carbs 65.2g | Sugar 8.7g | Protein 26g | Salt 1.4g

LF FENNEL, DOLCELATTE AND ROSEMARY PIZZA

That little bit more recherché than a Margherita, fennel, blue cheese and rosemary make for a refined union – and some black olives would not go amiss. Dolcelatte is that much gentler and sweeter than Gorgonzola, and as blue cheeses go it's on the pale side, so this is not overly pungent. If you are able to buy a frozen pizza base, this makes a good shortcut.

Serves 4

FOR THE PIZZA DOUGH
300g strong white bread flour, plus extra for dusting and kneading
½ teaspoon dried yeast
½ teaspoon caster sugar
1 heaped teaspoon sea salt
1 tablespoon extra virgin olive oil
150–175ml lukewarm water

TO TOP
2 fennel bulbs, shoots and tough outer sheath removed, fronds reserved and coarsely chopped
3 tablespoons extra virgin olive oil, plus extra for brushing
sea salt, black pepper
150g Dolcelatte, diced
1 tablespoon rosemary needles

Put the flour, yeast, sugar and sea salt in a large bowl. Add the olive oil, then gradually add enough of the lukewarm water until you have a workable dough. Knead on a lightly floured work surface for 8–10 minutes until smooth and elastic, or alternatively use an electric mixer or food processor with the dough attachment, in which case halve the time. Place in a lightly floured bowl, cut a cross in the top and sprinkle over a little more flour. Loosely cover with a clean tea towel and set aside in a warm draught-free spot for 1–3 hours until double in volume.

For the topping, halve the fennel bulbs downwards and finely slice across. Heat a couple of tablespoons of the olive oil in a medium saucepan over a low heat, add the fennel, season and gently fry for about 10 minutes until softened and translucent, stirring occasionally. This can be done well in advance.

Preheat the oven to 200°C fan/220°C/gas mark 7. Punch the dough down, sprinkling it with flour, and knead for a minute or two. Flatten and roll the dough into an oval about 27 × 37cm, shaping the edges with your fingers.* Transfer this to a baking sheet, brush with olive oil, spread the fennel over the base within the rim, scatter over the Dolcelatte and rosemary needles and drizzle with oil. Bake for 20 minutes until golden and sizzling. Serve hot or warm, drizzled with a little extra oil and scattered with the chopped fennel fronds, if wished.

*For a slightly spongier crust, leave to sit for 20 minutes before dressing.

SOURCE OF FOLATE, CALCIUM, PHOSPHOROUS
Energy 528 Kcal | Fat 24.7g | Sat fat 9.5g | Carbs 55.9g | Sugar 2.7g | Protein 17.8g | Salt 2.9g

LF CHEDDAR AND CHUTNEY MELT

It's hard to top this way of cooking a toastie. The bread is buttered and griddled in a frying pan, which makes for the toastiest, crispiest melt you can imagine. So play around with the cheese, and equally it could be ham instead of or as well as chutney. Throw a little salad into the equation somewhere for the contrast.

Serves 2

1 teaspoon softened unsalted butter
2 thick slices coarse-textured day-old white bread
70g cheddar, sliced
1 tablespoon chutney

Butter the bread on both sides. Cover one slice with the cheese, then spread with the chutney. Close the sandwich with the second piece of bread; it can be prepared to this point in advance.

Heat a non-stick frying pan over a high heat for several minutes. Place the sandwich in the pan, turn the heat down to medium–low and cook for 4–5 minutes on each side until golden on the outside and oozing melted cheese. Cut the toasted sandwich into four and arrange with the cut edges showing.

HIGH IN VITS D, B12, CALCIUM, PHOSPHOROUS | SOURCE OF VIT A, ZINC
Energy 272 Kcal | Fat 15.1g | Sat fat 9.1g | Carbs 20.7g | Sugar 3.2g | Protein 12.8g | Salt 1.4g

PARMA HAM AND GOAT'S CHEESE ON TOAST

This recipe makes a star out of an otherwise ordinary goat's cheese. In truth, melting does favours for many slightly dull cheeses. And visa versa: a fine mature cheese that has been lovingly finished might prove too forceful melted. A young Camembert is better for baking, for instance, than a really ripe one.

This makes for an open-faced melt. If you pop it onto a thick slice of toast. But the cheese is also lovely with a salad or some roast veg; thick slices of roast aubergine would make a perfect base.

Serves 4

2 sage leaves
2 × 100g medium-mature goat's cheeses, e.g. Capricorn
2 slices Parma or other air-dried ham
1 tablespoon extra virgin olive oil
watercress (enough for 4)
4 thick slices sourdough bread, or 8 slices sourdough baton, toasted

Lay a sage leaf on top of each goat's cheese, lay a slice of ham on top and tuck the ends underneath. Heat a teaspoon of the oil in a large non-stick frying pan over a low heat and fry the goat's cheeses for about 5 minutes either side, top first, until the ham is lightly golden and crisp – the cheese inside should be lovely and molten when you cut into it. Serve these (and the watercress drizzled with oil) with thick slices of toasted sourdough, also drizzled with oil.

HIGH IN VITS A, K | SOURCE OF VIT C, CALCIUM, PHOSPHOROUS, MANGANESE, IODINE
Energy 301 Kcal | Fat 17.3g | Sat fat 9.8g | Carbs 19.0g | Sugar 1.7g | Protein 16.4g | Salt 1.7g

FRENCH TOASTIE

Double delight: French toast married with a melt. I like to pile it with a salad of tomatoes, something very basic – halve and season some cherry tomatoes with salt and set aside while you are making the sarnie. But otherwise a pile of peppery green leaves. It is quite filling, so if the brakes are working it should do for two, but a hearty appetite will probably be able to take care of the whole thing.

Serves 2

1 medium free-range egg
2 tablespoons skimmed milk
sea salt, black pepper
2 tablespoons rapeseed or olive oil
2 large thick slices coarse-textured day-old white bread
50g raclette, thinly sliced
grainy mustard
2 cocktail gherkins, thinly sliced
1 teaspoon runny honey

Whisk the egg with the milk and some seasoning in a shallow bowl. Heat a tablespoon of the oil in a large non-stick frying pan over a medium heat. Dip one side of a slice of bread into the egg and milk mixture and fry for 2–3 minutes, dipped-side down, until golden, then place, fried-side up, on a board. Repeat with the second slice.

Turn the heat down a little. Lay the raclette over one of the slices, smear with mustard and scatter over the gherkins, then sandwich with the other piece, again cooked side to cheese. Now dip the sandwich on both sides in the egg and milk mixture, carefully turning it using a spatula. Add the remaining oil to the pan with the honey and fry for about 1½ minutes on each side until golden and the cheese has melted. Move it around a little to colour it evenly, and don't worry about the honey turning dark outside the sandwich, the idea is for the bread to turn deliciously golden and caramelised. Cut into triangles to serve.

HIGH IN CALCIUM | SOURCE OF VIT B12, PHOSPHOROUS, SELENIUM
Energy 376 Kcal | Fat 22.6g | Sat fat 7.4g | Carbs 27.9g | Sugar 5.2g | Protein 14.6g | Salt 1.5g

COMTÉ FONDUE WITH DIPPERS

Fondue is a dish that can sink the boat: it is almost impossible to stop dipping into that big pot of molten sin once you start. So coming up with a respectable alternative that didn't eat up a month's worth of saturated fat in one sitting has been simmering at the back of my mind throughout the writing of this book. And the only fault, I hope, that you will find with this elementary knock-together is that it would be quite nice to have another one. If you do, it is still within a day's healthy eating. It's a doddle to make, well within the remit of poached eggs on toast, and it makes for a fab supper. Add in some cooked spinach and you have Eggs Benedict.

Green asparagus has become a year-round feature in British food stores, but there is a window of April and May when thick white spears take up residence next to the green, and the two together make for a lovely duo with slightly different flavours and textures. But it could of course be the green on its own. There is also a stable of cheeses to choose from that will be just as gorgeous and melty as the Comté – Abondance, gruyère, Emmental and raclette are all contenders.

Serves 2

FOR THE FONDUE
2 teaspoons cornflour
150ml skimmed milk
½ teaspoon Dijon mustard
freshly grated nutmeg
60g Comté, finely diced
1 tablespoon finely snipped chives
2 teaspoons grated Parmesan

FOR THE DIPPERS
300g finger-thick green and white asparagus
12 quail eggs, boiled for 2½ minutes, shelled and halved
celery salt
2 chunks sourdough bread

In advance of making the fondue, bring a large pan of salted water to the boil.

Trim the asparagus spears where they become visibly woody, and peel the stalk within 1–2cm of the beginning of the tip.

Blend the cornflour with a couple of tablespoons of the milk in a small bowl.

Heat the grill. Bring the remaining milk to the boil in a small non-stick saucepan, stir in the cornflour mixture and stir continuously until the sauce thickens, then remove from the heat. Whisk in the mustard and season with nutmeg. Stir in the Comté and the chives, spread over the base of two small shallow ovenproof bowls, scatter over the Parmesan and pop under the grill for about 5 minutes until golden and toasty.

Put the asparagus into the pan of boiling water at the same time as grilling the fondue and cook for 4–5 minutes until the thickest part of a spear slices with ease. Drain the spears into a colander.

Serve the fondue with the asparagus, the quail eggs, celery salt and bread for scooping.

HIGH IN FOLATE | SOURCE OF VIT B2, CALCIUM, PHOSPHOROUS
Energy 458 Kcal | Fat 23.5g | Sat fat 10.4g | Carbs 27.4g | Sugar 7g | Protein 31.9g | Salt 1.2g

THREE CHEESE AND TOMATO MUFFINS

One for cheese bread addicts, without the hassle of yeast cookery. So good eaten warm when the little pockets of cheese are gooey, a mélange of Emmental and gruyère, but otherwise Comté or Abondance, and the pecorino could be Parmesan. They will be there on demand for several days thereafter stored in an airtight bag, and will come back to life given 10 minutes in an oven heated to 170°C fan/190°C/gas mark 5.

Makes 12*

250g plain flour
50g ground almonds
50g pecorino, finely grated
1 tablespoon baking powder
pinch of sea salt
3 medium free-range eggs
225ml whole milk
5 tablespoons extra virgin olive oil
8 sun-dried tomato halves in oil, drained and finely chopped
100g Emmental, cut into 1cm dice
100g gruyère, cut into 1cm dice
2 tablespoons pesto
1 heaped tablespoon coarsely snipped chives

Preheat the oven to 200°C fan/220°C/gas mark 7, and line a 12-hole muffin tin with paper cases; alternatively, butter and line the base with paper. Combine the flour, ground almonds, pecorino, baking powder and salt in a large bowl. Whisk the eggs and milk in another large bowl, then stir in the olive oil. Pour this mixture onto the dry ingredients and mix to a lumpy batter. Fold in the sun-dried tomatoes. Combine the two cheeses, set aside about a quarter and fold in the remainder. Dot with the pesto and gently fold over a few times to streak the mixture. Divide between the paper cases, filling them to within 1cm of the top. Place a couple of cubes of the reserved cheese in the very centre of each muffin, then scatter over a pinch of chives.

Bake for 10 minutes, then turn the oven down to 170°C fan/190°C/gas mark 5 and bake for a further 15 minutes. Serve them warm or newly cooled.

*The mixture makes at least 12 muffins, but depending on the size of your moulds, you may get a few more.

HIGH IN VITS E, B12, CALCIUM, PHOSPHOROUS | SOURCE OF VITS A, B2, ZINC
Energy 299 Kcal | Fat 20.1g | Sat fat 6.2g | Carbs 17.2g | Sugar 1.5g | Protein 11.9g | Salt 0.8g

LF METRO CHILLI QUESADILLAS

Quesadillas take over where toasted sarnies leave off, embracing all the punchy Tex-Mex flavours that a couple of slices of white will never be able to. After some canvassing of nearest and dearest about what exactly should go into the quesadilla of their dreams, this is the combo that came up. Dipping the gooey little pockets into a slushy guacamole is very much a part of the ritual; the Avocado, Coriander and Lime Dip on page 78 is also a goer.

Serves 2

4 small tortillas
120g sliced Leerdammer (6 thin slices)
100g thinly sliced roast guinea fowl or free-range chicken
2 teaspoons chilli jam
1 spring onion, trimmed and thinly sliced
3–4 slices Parma or other air-dried ham

Heat a frying pan, ideally cast-iron, over a medium–low heat for 4–5 minutes. Lay the tortillas out on a board and cover them with the cheese. Scatter the guinea fowl or chicken over two of the tortillas, then drizzle over the chilli jam and scatter with the spring onion. Lay the Parma ham over the remaining two, then carefully turn these on top of the other tortillas to make quesadillas, and gently press down.

Dry-fry the quesadillas for 3 minutes either side or until lightly golden and gooey in the centre. Cut into quarters and serve with guacamole (see below).

*These quesadillas can be made well in advance on the day, and wrapped in clingfilm and chilled until required.

HIGH IN CALCIUM, PHOSPHOROUS | SOURCE OF VITS B3, B12, ZINC
Energy 541 Kcal | Fat 24.7g | Sat fat 13.2g | Carbs 37.8g | Sugar 4.4g | Protein 40.8g | Salt 2.3g

GUACAMOLE

Serves 4

2 avocados, halved, stoned and flesh scooped out
1 tablespoon coarsely chopped red onion
½ teaspoon finely chopped medium–hot red chilli
1 tablespoon coarsely chopped coriander
1 tablespoon lemon or lime juice
1 tablespoon extra virgin olive oil, plus extra to serve
sea salt
cayenne pepper, for dusting

Whizz all the ingredients to a purée in a food processor, transfer to a serving bowl, cover with clingfilm and chill for up to half a day. Drizzle with a little olive oil and dust with cayenne pepper to serve.

SOURCE OF VITS E, B6, FIBRE, POTASSIUM
Energy 128 Kcal | Fat 12.6g | Sat fat 2.5g | Carbs 1.4g | Sugar 0.6g | Protein 1.1g | Salt trace

GRAINS & PASTA

SPINACH AND RICOTTA GNOCCHI

These tender green dumplings or gnocchi are a personal favourite. A fair bit of work, but nothing too arduous when you are in cruise mode over the weekend. The recipe comes together in stages, so you can cook the spinach and go and do something else, and then make up the mixture, and roll and poach the dumplings at the last minute.

Gnocchi is another dish where the fat counter can run away if you allow it, what with all that ricotta and Parmesan, smothered in butter and more Parmesan. I don't think there is any stinting to be done with the dumpling itself. Ricotta is a whey cheese with a firm curd that holds its own under heat, unlike say a young goat's cheese, which might melt. But hold the butter; a handful of sage leaves lightly fried in olive oil with a few drops of lemon juice will be every bit as good.

Serves 4

900g–1kg spinach leaves, washed
200g ricotta, drained
4 medium free-range egg yolks
sea salt, black pepper
freshly grated nutmeg
½ teaspoon finely grated lemon zest, plus a generous squeeze of lemon juice
10g cornflour
50g Parmesan, freshly grated, plus extra to serve
plain flour for dusting
3 tablespoons extra virgin olive oil, plus extra to serve
couple of handfuls of sage or basil leaves

You will need to cook the spinach in two goes. Pile half into a large saucepan, cover with a lid and cook over a low heat for 10–15 minutes until wilted, stirring and pushing it down halfway through. Drain this into a colander and cook the remainder, then drain this too and leave to cool completely for about 1½ hours.

Squeeze out as much liquid from the spinach as possible using your hands, and then, to dry it out further, squeeze it half at a time in a clean tea towel.

Blend the ricotta and egg yolks in a large bowl, then whisk until smooth and add some seasoning, a little nutmeg and the lemon zest and cornflour. Add the spinach, teasing out the lumps, and blend, then stir in the Parmesan. Cover and chill for several hours when the mixture will firm up a little.

Bring a large pan of salted water to the boil. Place some flour in a shallow soup bowl or on a plate. Gently shape teaspoons of the spinach and ricotta mixture into a dumpling, then drop them into the flour and carefully turn to coat them, and set aside. This needs to be done close to the time of cooking, as they will absorb the flour.

Lower the dumplings into the water using a slotted spatula and poach over a low heat for about 4 minutes or until they rise to the surface. Remove them using a slotted utensil and divide between four warmed shallow soup bowls.

While the dumplings are poaching, heat the oil in a large frying pan over a medium heat, scatter the herb leaves over the oil, gently press to submerge and fry briefly until crisp and a very pale gold. Spoon these and the oil over the dumplings. Drizzle over a little more oil, squeeze over a little lemon juice, then dust with Parmesan.

HIGH IN VITS A, K, FOLATE | SOURCE OF VITS C, B12, POTASSIUM, CALCIUM, PHOSPHOROUS, IRON, MANGANESE Energy 364 Kcal | Fat 25.2g | Sat fat 8.9g | Carbs 11g | Sugar 4.7g | Protein 19.8g | Salt 1.3g

SPICY SPELT PILAF WITH SAFFRON YOGURT

Friends in kind, pearled spelt takes over where pearl barley leaves off, though I would say spelt has the edge with its polish and finish; it's not as starchy. This is a great basic, which you can serve on its own with a dollop of the yogurt and a leafy green salad.

Serves 4

FOR THE PILAF
3 tablespoons groundnut or vegetable oil
4 shallots, peeled and thinly sliced
1 cinnamon stick
8 green cardamom pods, smashed
4 cloves
2 bay leaves
2 strips of lemon zest (removed with a potato peeler)
250g pearled spelt, rinsed
450ml chicken stock or water
1 teaspoon Maldon sea salt
50g roasted cashew nuts
small coriander and mint leaves, to serve

Heat the oil in a medium saucepan over a medium heat, add the shallots, spices, bay leaves and lemon zest and fry for 3–5 minutes until lightly coloured, stirring frequently. Stir in the spelt, add the stock and salt, bring to the boil, skimming off any foam that rises to the surface initially, and simmer for 17 minutes until almost all the liquid has been absorbed.

Clamp on a lid, turn off the heat and leave for 20 minutes. It's not a bad idea to fish out the cardamom pods and cloves, but the rest of the aromatics are easy enough to spot while eating, then fluff it up with a fork. This pilaf is quite good-natured and if you leave it a little longer than 20 minutes it won't come to any harm. Fold in the nuts and serve scattered with coriander and mint leaves, accompanied by the yogurt (see below).

FOR THE SAFFRON YOGURT
150g 0%-fat Greek yogurt
1 tablespoon soured cream
1 teaspoon lemon juice, plus ½ teaspoon finely grated zest
small pinch of saffron filaments (about 10), ground and
   infused in 1 teaspoon boiling water
½ teaspoon sumac
sea salt

Mix all the ingredients together in a small bowl. You can do this while the pilaf is cooking or, even better, in advance, then cover and chill to allow the flavours to develop.

Energy 421 Kcal | Fat 17.0g | Sat fat 2.9g | Carbs 48.7g | Sugar 8.5g | Protein 14.6g | Salt 1.9g

BROCCOLI AND QUINOA PILAF WITH CRISPY FETA

This oven-baked pilaf is scented with spices and finished with a punchy harissa. Cooking feta this way may seem unlikely, and don't worry if at first it looks as though it might collapse in the pan; the end result is divinely gooey on the inside with lots of crispy bits on the outside.

Serves 6

5 tablespoons extra virgin olive oil
3 banana shallots, peeled, halved lengthways and thinly sliced across
2 long red peppers, cores and seeds discarded, thickly sliced across
2 garlic cloves, peeled and finely chopped
1 heaped teaspoon ground coriander
1 heaped teaspoon ground cumin
300g quinoa (ideally tricolor)
600ml vegetable stock
1 cinnamon stick
sea salt
200g cherry tomatoes, halved or quartered
200g long-stem broccoli, ends trimmed and sliced into 1cm lengths
1 tablespoon lemon juice
1 heaped teaspoon harissa
200g block of feta*, drained on kitchen paper
handful of coarsely chopped flat-leaf parsley

Preheat the oven to 180°C fan/200°C/gas mark 6. Heat 2 tablespoons of the olive oil in a large cast-iron casserole over a medium heat and fry the shallots and peppers for about 5 minutes until softened, then stir in the garlic, coriander and cumin and fry for another couple of minutes until starting to colour, stirring frequently. Stir in the quinoa and cook for 1 minute or until it begins to pop. Pour in the stock, add the cinnamon stick, very lightly season with salt and bring to the boil, then cover and cook in the oven for 15 minutes. Scatter over the tomatoes and the broccoli and return to the oven for a further 20 minutes, then gently stir the vegetables into the quinoa and cook for another 10 minutes or until the quinoa and broccoli are tender.

In the meantime, blend the lemon juice and harissa in a small bowl, then stir in a couple of tablespoons of the oil.

When you return the pilaf to the oven for the final 10 minutes, heat a small non-stick frying pan over a medium heat, add the remaining tablespoon of oil and fry the block of feta for 5 minutes until golden and crusty – you will find it oozes a bit, but this should turn nice and crispy, so don't worry about the appearance. Carefully turn using a spatula, scraping the crispy bits on top, and cook for a further 5 minutes.

Scatter the parsley over the pilaf and gently mix in. Slice the feta, then break up with a fork and serve dotted over the pilaf, drizzled with the harissa oil.

*A basic block of feta will be better here than a pukka barrel-aged cheese: the firmer the better.

HIGH IN VITS K, C | SOURCE OF VIT A
Energy 373 Kcal | Fat 19.7g | Sat fat 6.3g | Carbs 32.4g | Sugar 8.2g | Protein 15.1g | Salt 2g

LF SPELT AND HAZELNUT-STUFFED MUSHROOMS

Both Portobello or the large, floppy flat-cap mushrooms will lend themselves to being stuffed, or perhaps I should say 'filled' for fear of losing you to one of 'life's too short to…s'. The dairy in this instance is a little butter, which makes all the difference by bringing out the flavour of the mushrooms, and olive oil takes care of the rest. This makes a good veggie main, but equally these mushrooms would be at home with an autumnal beef or venison stew or roast. And you can vary the nuts: toasted macadamia and Brazil nuts are ever delicious.

Serves 4

125g pearled spelt
8 medium flat-cap mushrooms
4 garlic cloves, peeled and finely chopped
3 tablespoons extra virgin olive oil
30g unsalted butter
sea salt, black pepper
2 banana shallots, peeled and finely chopped
150g button mushrooms, stalks trimmed and thinly sliced
finely grated zest of 1 lemon, plus 1 tablespoon of juice
2 tablespoons coarsely chopped flat-leaf parsley
2 tablespoons snipped dill
30g hazelnuts, toasted and chopped, to serve

Bring a medium pan of salted water to the boil, add the spelt and simmer for 17–20 minutes until tender, then drain into a sieve.

In the meantime, preheat the oven to 180°C fan/200°C/gas mark 6. Trim the flat-cap mushroom stalks level with the cups, and arrange them, cup-side up, in one or two roasting pans. Divide the garlic between the cups, drizzle over 2 tablespoons of the olive oil, dot with half the butter, season and bake for 25 minutes.

Five minutes before the mushrooms come out of the oven, heat the remaining oil and butter in a large non-stick frying pan over a medium heat and fry the shallots for a couple of minutes, stirring frequently, until softened and just starting to colour. Add the button mushrooms, season and continue to fry for several minutes until lightly coloured. Stir in the spelt and lemon zest and heat through. Stir in the herbs and lemon juice and taste for seasoning. Divide this between the mushrooms, and scatter over the hazelnuts. These are good eaten hot or warm.

SOURCE OF VITS B2, B3, B5, B7, FOLATE
Energy 369 Kcal | Fat 21.3g | Sat fat 5.8g | Carbs 23.9g | Sugar 3.5g | Protein 16.3g | Salt 0.2g

LINGUINE WITH PESTO AND BRAZIL NUT PANGRATTATO

This zesty pesto has strains of mint and parsley as well as basil, and the toasted Brazil nuts make a fine alternative to *pangrattato* (an Italian take on breadcrumbs) with their inimitable buttery quality. There are lots of gluten-free pastas on the market if you want to go down that route.

Serves 4

FOR THE PASTA
75g Brazil nuts, quite finely chopped
2 red onions, peeled, halved and thinly sliced across
1 tablespoon extra virgin olive oil
1 teaspoon balsamic vinegar
300g linguine or spaghetti
75g medium-mature goat's cheese, crumbled

FOR THE PESTO
30g mint leaves
30g basil leaves
30g flat-leaf parsley
1 garlic clove, peeled
3 tablespoons extra virgin olive oil
50g Parmesan, freshly grated
sea salt, black pepper

Preheat the oven to 180°C fan/200°C/gas mark 6. Spread out the nuts on a non-stick baking sheet and toast on the lower shelf for 8–10 minutes until a pale even gold. Leave to cool. At the same time as toasting the nuts, spread out the onions in a thin layer on another non-stick baking sheet, breaking the slices into rings as far as possible. Drizzle over the oil and toss to coat them. Roast for 30–35 minutes on the shelf above the nuts, stirring after 20 minutes to ensure that they caramelise evenly. Pick out any stray burnt strands, then drizzle over the vinegar and stir to coat.

In the meantime, whizz the herbs with the garlic in a food processor until finely chopped, then gradually pour in the olive oil through the funnel with the motor running. Add the Parmesan and some seasoning and give it a quick whizz (this can also be prepared well in advance).

Bring a large pan of salted water to the boil, add the pasta and give it a stir to separate out the strands, then simmer until just tender, according to the packet instructions. Drain into a colander, leaving it on the wet side, then return it to the saucepan. Add the pesto and toss, then gently fold in the goat's cheese, which will melt with the residual heat. Divide between four warm plates, place a pile of the crispy onions on top and scatter over the nuts.

HIGH IN VIT K, PHOSPHOROUS, SELENIUM | SOURCE OF VIT B1, CALCIUM, MAGNESIUM, IRON, ZINC, MANGANESE Energy 635 Kcal | Fat 34.0g | Sat fat 10.8g | Carbs 57.2g | Sugar 4.9g | Protein 22.5 g | Salt 0.5 g

LF TAGLIATELLE WITH ROAST ASPARAGUS

Asparagus has great presence, and infuses a dish of pasta with little call for anything else aside from a generous addition of Parmesan and some parsley. Enjoy the minimalism.

Serves 4

350–400g thin asparagus, ends trimmed, and cut into 3–4cm pieces
2 tablespoons extra virgin olive oil
sea salt, black pepper
3 garlic cloves, peeled and finely chopped
1 teaspoon finely chopped medium–hot red chilli
300g tagliatelle
2 tablespoons lemon juice
50g Parmesan, freshly grated, plus extra, finely shaved, to serve
2 handfuls of coarsely chopped flat-leaf parsley

Preheat the oven to 190°C fan/210°C/gas mark 6½. Arrange the asparagus in a crowded layer in a large roasting pan, drizzle over the olive oil, season and toss to coat. Roast for 15 minutes, then stir in the garlic and chilli and continue to roast for another 10 minutes until really soft and lightly coloured.

Meanwhile, bring a large pan of salted water to the boil. Add the pasta, give it a stir to separate out the strands and simmer until just tender, according to the packet instructions. Reserving half a teacup of the cooking liquid, drain the pasta into a colander, then tip it into the asparagus roasting pan, drizzle over the lemon juice and scatter over the Parmesan and a little more seasoning. Drizzle over the reserved cooking liquid, place the pan over a gentle heat and stir constantly until the pasta is coated in a creamy emulsion. Stir in the parsley and serve scattered with fine shavings of Parmesan.

HIGH IN FOLATE | SOURCE OF VITS K, C, B1, PHOSPHORUS, MANGANESE
Energy 404 Kcal | Fat 11.2g | Sat fat 3.4g | Carbs 55.6g | Sugar 4.4g | Protein 17.4g | Salt 0.3g

LF VERY TOMATOEY MAC 'N' CHEESE

Most of us would sell our souls for a bowl of mac 'n' cheese, happily disregarding good intentions. So I hope that this alternative version in which a tomato sauce replaces the usual rich white one will win friends. You still get generous pockets of gooey cheese, and a lovely crispy top, but it is altogether fresher. The gold standard here involves making your own slow-cooked sauce, and I would up the quantity, as it freezes beautifully. But otherwise, a couple of tubs of a good ready-made tomato sauce will still turn out a decent mac 'n' cheese.

Serves 6

SPEEDY

300g macaroni
2 × 350g tubs (or 700g) fresh Napoletana tomato sauce
75g sun-dried tomatoes, coarsely chopped
175g gruyère, cut into thin strips a few centimetres long
150g cocktail tomatoes, quartered
1 tablespoon extra virgin olive oil
sea salt, black pepper
25g Parmesan, freshly grated

Bring a large pan of salted water to the boil, and preheat the oven to 190°C fan/210°C/ gas mark 6½. Add the macaroni to the pan, give it a stir and cook until almost tender, then drain it into a colander and return it to the pan. Toss with the tomato sauce and mix in the sun-dried tomatoes and the gruyère. Transfer to a 30cm oval gratin or other similar-sized ovenproof dish. You could also make it in large individual bowls, so each one serves two. Toss the cocktail tomatoes with the oil and seasoning and scatter over, then top with the Parmesan. Bake for 30–35 minutes until golden and sizzling.

HIGH IN VIT D | SOURCE OF VITS A, E, CALCIUM, PHOSPHORUS
Energy 513 Kcal | Fat 26.6g | Sat fat 10.2g | Carbs 47.1g | Sugar 6.6g | Protein 19.1g | Salt 1.9g

SLOWLY DOES IT

1kg vine tomatoes, quartered
30g unsalted butter
4 tablespoons extra virgin olive oil
sea salt, black pepper
300g macaroni
75g sun-dried tomatoes, coarsely chopped
200g Comté, cut into thin strips a few centimetres long
150g cocktail tomatoes, quartered
25g Parmesan, freshly grated

Place the tomatoes in a medium saucepan, cover and cook over a low heat for 20–30 minutes, stirring them occasionally, until they collapse. Pass through a sieve or a mouli-légumes and return to the pan, washing it out if necessary. Add the butter, 3 tablespoons of the olive oil and some seasoning. Bring to the boil and simmer very gently, uncovered, for 35–40 minutes until thickened but still of a thin pouring consistency, stirring towards the end. The sauce can be prepared in advance, in which case cover and set aside.

Bring a large pan of salted water to the boil and preheat the oven to 190°C fan/210°C/gas mark 6½. Add the pasta to the pan, give it a stir and cook until almost tender, then drain it into a colander and return it to the pan. Toss with the sauce and mix in the sun-dried tomatoes and the Comté. Transfer to a 30cm oval gratin or other similar-sized ovenproof dish. Toss the cocktail tomatoes with the remaining oil and a little seasoning and scatter over, then top with the Parmesan. Bake for 30–35 minutes until golden and sizzling.

SOURCE OF VITS A, E, C, CALCIUM, PHOSPHOROUS
Energy 469 Kcal | Fat 23.7g | Sat fat 10.9g | Carbs 42.4g | Sugar 7.1g | Protein 19.3g | Salt 0.9g

RICCIOLI WITH LEMON AND CHILLI

Riccioli are endearing corkscrew spirals, though very skinny egg noodles come a close second for this dish. This feisty sauce makes for a speedy standby, up there with puttanesca. The Parmesan serves up a double whammy, both flavouring the sauce and emulsifying the juices into a creamy coating sauce.

Serves 4

finely grated zest and juice of 1 lemon
2 teaspoons finely chopped medium–hot red chilli
6 tablespoons extra virgin olive oil
sea salt
6 tablespoons coarsely chopped flat-leaf parsley
75g Parmesan, freshly grated, plus extra to serve
400g riccioli

Bring a large pan of salted water to the boil. Whisk the lemon zest and juice, chilli and olive oil in a large bowl with some salt, then stir in the parsley and the Parmesan. At the same time, add the pasta to the boiling water, give it a stir to separate out the spirals and simmer until just tender, according to the packet instructions, then drain it into a sieve or colander, but not too thoroughly, immediately add to the sauce and toss to coat. Serve with an extra sprinkling of Parmesan.

Cooking water Pasta continues to dry out in the minutes after it has drained, and a little moisture adds enormously to the coating consistency of the sauce. To this end, either reserve a teacup of the cooking liquid and add a drop to the pasta when you toss it, or simply drain it but not too thoroughly, adding it to the sauce while still trickling a few drops.

HIGH IN VITS K, C, IODINE | SOURCE OF VITS A, B12, CALCIUM, PHOSPHORUS, ZINC, MANGANESE, SELENIUM Energy 514 Kcal | Fat 24.8g | Sat fat 6g | Carbs 53.8g | Sugar 2.2g | Protein 18.3g | Salt 0.5g

LF FARFALLE WITH ROASTED TOMATOES AND GORGONZOLA

This kind of rustic fare underpins suppertime in our house; not a sauce as such, but a play on roasted veg, with Gorgonzola melted into the roasting juices; a tasty mélange to coat the pasta. Serve with a green salad or some wholemeal bread for mopping up any left over.

Serves 4

600g baby plum tomatoes
5 tablespoons extra virgin olive oil
1 tablespoon balsamic vinegar
300g farfalle or penne
150g Gorgonzola, cut into 1cm dice
large handful of basil leaves, torn
black pepper

Preheat the oven to 240°C fan/260°C/gas mark 9. Arrange the tomatoes in a large roasting pan, pour over 2 tablespoons of the oil and the balsamic vinegar and roast for 10 minutes. Meanwhile, bring a large pan of salted water to the boil. Add the pasta, give it a stir and cook until just tender, according to the packet instructions, then drain into a colander. Add the remaining ingredients to the pan, including the cooked pasta and some pepper, and gently toss, then return to the oven for 1 minute until the cheese is melting.

SOURCE OF VIT C, PHOSPHORUS
Energy 505 Kcal | Fat 28.5g | Sat fat 9.9g | Carbs 44.2g | Sugar 5.4g | Protein 16.9g | Salt 1.7g

LF SPINACH AND ANCHOVY BULGAR-OTTO

A lively risotto, as befits this grain; lots of garlic, chilli and anchovy give it a kick, and it is light and clean by comparison to most. It is an excellent one for serving with lamb chops. Marinate 8 cutlets in 2 tablespoons each of lemon juice and extra virgin olive oil with a tablespoon of thyme leaves for about 1 hour. Heat a ridged griddle pan over a medium–high heat, season and grill for about 2 minutes on each side. In this case you may prefer to keep the risotto on the dry side, by reducing the stock to 1 litre.

Serves 4

1 tablespoon extra virgin olive oil
25g unsalted butter
4 garlic cloves, peeled and finely chopped
1 heaped teaspoon finely sliced red chilli
8 anchovy fillets, sliced
300g bulgar wheat
150ml white wine
1.2 litres chicken stock
5 cocktail plum tomatoes, quartered
300g baby spinach leaves
2 spring onions, trimmed and cut into thin slivers 5cm long (optional)
lemon wedges, to serve

Preheat the oven to 180°C fan/200°C/gas mark 6. Heat the olive oil and the butter in a large cast-iron casserole over a medium heat, add the garlic, chilli and anchovy and gently cook until fragrant and the anchovies have melted. Add the bulgar and stir for about 1 minute, then add the wine and simmer until this has been absorbed. Add the stock, bring to the boil, cover and cook in the oven for 20 minutes.

Stir in the tomatoes and spinach, and return to the oven for a further 5 minutes. Serve scattered with spring onions if wished, accompanied by lemon wedges.

HIGH IN VIT K | SOURCE OF VIT A
Energy 408 Kcal | Fat 10.8g | Sat fat 3.8g | Carbs 57.7g | Sugar 2.3g | Protein 12.6g | Salt 2g

A NEW LOOK AT SAUCES:
ROASTS, GRILLS & STEWS

MEXICAN SMOKY CHICKEN AND PEPPER STEW

Dried ancho chilli provides a smoky savoury hit in this juicy chicken stew, with lots of paprika and red peppers that work in unison. The flavours are clean and sharp; soured cream is a natural consort, softening the juices without being remotely rich.

Serves 4

FOR THE STEW
1 dried ancho chilli
sea salt, black pepper
1.4–1.6kg free-range chicken thighs and drumsticks
2 tablespoons extra virgin olive oil
1 large onion, peeled and chopped
2 long red peppers, cores and seeds removed, cut into thin strips 5–7cm long
3 garlic cloves, peeled and finely sliced
1 teaspoon sweet paprika
1 teaspoon ground cumin
1 teaspoon dried mint or oregano
400g can chopped tomatoes

TO SERVE
4 teaspoons soured cream
4 tablespoons diced avocado
coarsely chopped coriander

Place the ancho chilli in a small bowl, cover with boiling water and soak for 20 minutes, turning it over halfway through. Drain, pull out the core and coarsely chop, discarding the seeds. Set aside.

Heat a large cast-iron casserole over a medium heat, and season the chicken pieces on each side. Add a tablespoon of the oil to the pan and colour the chicken on both sides, working in batches, removing the pieces to a bowl as you go. Tip out the fat, add the remaining tablespoon of oil, turn the heat down a little and fry the onion and peppers for 6–8 minutes until starting to colour, stirring occasionally. Stir in the garlic, spices, mint or oregano and chopped chilli and fry for a further couple of minutes until fragrant and lightly golden. Add the canned tomatoes, and stir the chicken into the sauce, pressing the pieces down to almost cover them. Bring to a simmer, then cover and cook over a low heat for 1 hour, turning the pieces halfway through.

Divide the chicken between warm plates or shallow bowls, skim the excess oil off the surface of the sauce, taste and, if wished, simmer to reduce and concentrate the flavour a little before ladling it over the chicken. Serve with a dollop of soured cream, some diced avocado and chopped coriander scattered over.

SOURCE OF VITS C, B3
Energy 546 Kcal | Fat 35.3g | Sat fat 9.1g | Carbs 12.8g | Sugar 9.3g | Protein 42.2g | Salt 0.4g

ROAST CHICKEN WITH CIDER GRAVY

Many of my best memories of roast chicken revolve around the generous river of creamy gravy that surrounded those thin slices of breast. So I wanted to jot down a way of achieving that which is not overly rich – just a little crème fraîche in with the cider and roasting juices is all that it takes.

Serves 4

FOR THE CHICKEN
25g unsalted butter, softened
1 × 1.6kg free-range chicken, untrussed
sea salt, black pepper
1 tablespoon soft thyme leaves
200ml medium–dry cider
50g crème fraîche
1 teaspoon plain flour blended with 1 teaspoon unsalted butter

FOR THE BROCCOLI AND APPLE
2 banana shallots, peeled, halved lengthways and thinly sliced across
400–450g longstem broccoli, stalks trimmed and sliced 1cm thick
1 cooking apple (200–250g), peeled, quartered, cored and cut into 1cm dice
squeeze of lemon juice
15g unsalted butter
1 tablespoon rapeseed oil
handful of coarsely chopped flat-leaf parsley

Preheat the oven to 190°C fan/210°C/gas mark 6½. Smear the butter over the chicken in a roasting pan that holds it snugly. Season and scatter over the thyme, then roast for 50 minutes.

About 15 minutes before the chicken comes out of the oven, start to cook the broccoli. Prepare the vegetables and the apple, tossing it with a squeeze of lemon juice in a bowl. Heat the butter and oil in a large saucepan over a medium heat and fry the shallot for 1–2 minutes until it softens, stirring frequently, then add the apple and cook for a couple of minutes longer. Add the broccoli and stir until coated in the oil, season and add 100ml water. Cover and simmer for 8–10 minutes or until almost tender, stirring halfway through. Stir again, turn the heat up and cook, uncovered, for a further few minutes or until the excess liquid evaporates. Taste for seasoning and stir in the parsley.

Transfer the chicken to a warm plate to rest for 15 minutes, tipping any juices inside the cavity back into the pan. Skim the excess fat off the roasting juices, add the cider and simmer to reduce by half, scraping up the sticky residue. Add the crème fraîche and simmer vigorously for a couple of minutes. Add 100ml water and bring to a simmer, then add the butter and flour paste in nibs and cook for a minute or so longer. You can also add any juices given out on resting the bird. Taste for seasoning and strain into a bowl or jug. Carve and serve the chicken with the broccoli and apple, and the gravy.

HIGH IN VIT K | SOURCE OF VIT C
Energy 591 Kcal | Fat 42.9g | Sat fat 16.1g | Carbs 9.2g | Sugar 7.6g | Protein 36.2g | Salt 0.4g

CHICKEN AND SPELT WITH BUTTERMILK SAUCE

The star here is the buttermilk and chia seed sauce – a revival in fortunes for one, and a debut for the other. The unique talent of chia seeds is to thicken a liquid medium, hence the popular porridge. This knack can also be employed in savoury dishes in all manner of ways. Buttermilk, for instance, is too thin as a sauce in its own right, but acquires a deliciously gloopy texture with the addition of a few chia seeds.

The chicken and veggies are an all-in-one – leeks and red onions roast down to a gorgeously silky mass, with chicken breasts to flavour the juices, and pearled spelt stirred in at the end. You can buy spelt ready-cooked in a pouch if it is easier.

Serves 4

FOR THE CHICKEN AND SPELT
600g leeks (trimmed weight), thickly sliced
2 red onions, peeled, halved and thinly sliced
6 garlic cloves, peeled and halved lengthways
4 small rosemary sprigs
6–8 tablespoons extra virgin olive oil
sea salt, black pepper
150g pearled spelt
4 × 150–200g skinless free-range chicken breasts
1 tablespoon lemon juice, plus a generous squeeze
paprika, for dusting
4 tablespoons coarsely chopped flat-leaf parsley

FOR THE BUTTERMILK AND CHIA SEED SAUCE
100ml buttermilk
30g soured cream
1 small garlic clove, peeled and crushed to a paste
sea salt
1 heaped teaspoon chia seeds

Ideally make the sauce the night before, to allow the chia seeds to swell and thicken the sauce. It will still be good, however, made close to the time, when the seeds will be crunchy. Combine the buttermilk and soured cream in a small bowl, mix in the garlic and a little salt and stir through the chia seeds. Cover and chill until required.

Preheat the oven to 190°C fan/210°C/gas mark 6½. Combine the leeks, onions, garlic and rosemary in a large roasting pan, drizzle over 4 tablespoons of the oil, season and toss to coat. Roast for 30 minutes, stirring halfway through.

Towards the end of this time, bring a medium pan of salted water to the boil, add the spelt and simmer for 17–20 minutes until tender, then drain into a sieve.

In the meantime, cut out the white tendon, if visible, from the underside of each chicken breast. Toss the chicken breasts in a large bowl with 2 tablespoons of the oil and the tablespoon of lemon juice, and season each side with sea salt and a light dusting of paprika. Heat a large non-stick frying pan over a medium heat, and colour the breasts on both sides in two batches.

Give the vegetables a stir, tuck the chicken breasts in between and roast for a further 15 minutes. Transfer the chicken to a plate, discard the rosemary sprigs and stir the spelt into the vegetables, then drizzle over another couple of tablespoons of oil if wished. Season with salt and a generous squeeze of lemon juice, scatter over the parsley and toss. Serve the chicken with the roasted veg spelt, accompanied by the sauce.

SOURCE OF VITS K, B3, B6
Energy 651 Kcal | Fat 28.4g | Sat fat 5.9g | Carbs 39.2g | Sugar 11.6g | Protein 53.8g | Salt 0.3g

CHICKEN MEATBALLS WITH TAHINI CREAM

A summery take on this genre, with chicken meatballs sitting within lightly braised courgettes and spring onions, and plenty of greenery to lift it. Once again, yogurt comes to the rescue to provide a note of luxury, blended with tahini.

Serves 4

FOR THE MEATBALLS
700g skinless free-range chicken thighs
4 tablespoons finely chopped flat-leaf parsley
2 shallots, peeled and finely chopped
sea salt, black pepper
4 tablespoons extra virgin olive oil

FOR THE TAHINI CREAM
50g tahini paste
50g low-fat Greek yogurt
2 tablespoons lemon juice
2–3 tablespoons water

FOR THE STEW
750g courgettes, ends trimmed, halved lengthways and thickly sliced
250g spring onions (about 2 bunches), trimmed and cut into thirds
4 garlic cloves, peeled and thinly sliced
70ml white wine
2 tablespoons water or stock
1 tablespoon lemon juice
10g dill, coarsely chopped, plus extra to serve
10g mint, coarsely chopped, plus extra to serve

Cut the chicken thighs into chunks and whizz to a pulp in a food processor. Transfer this to a bowl and add all the remaining ingredients for the meatballs, including a tablespoon of the oil. Shape the mixture into balls the size of a large walnut between your palms. Set aside on a couple of plates, cover and chill until required.

In the meantime, blend the tahini and yogurt in a small bowl, then work in the lemon juice, and enough water to achieve a thick drizzling consistency, and season with a little salt. The sauce can be made well in advance, in which case cover and chill until required.*

Heat a teaspoon of oil in a large non-stick frying pan and colour the meatballs in batches.

At the same time, heat a tablespoon of the oil in a large cast-iron casserole over a high heat and fry about one-third of the courgettes and spring onions for a few minutes, stirring frequently, until they start to colour. Transfer them to a bowl and cook the remaining vegetables in the same way, adding more oil to the pan with each batch, and adding the garlic about a minute before the very end.

Turn the heat down low, return all the vegetables to the pan and season them. Mix in the meatballs and pour over the wine and water or stock, which should come to the boil instantly, then cover and cook over a low heat for 10 minutes.

Stir in the lemon juice and the herbs. Serve with the tahini cream and some more herbs scattered over.

*If making the tahini cream in advance, you may need to add a drop more water to loosen it.

SOURCE OF VITS K, C, FOLATE
Energy 534 Kcal | Fat 29.3g | Sat fat 6.4g | Carbs 7.8g | Sugar 6.5g | Protein 54g | Salt 0.2g

CHICKEN WITH ZA'ATAR AND AUBERGINE YOGURT

This spicy tray-baked chicken comes with a baba ghanoush-style dip. I am afraid I can never be bothered to hover over a hot stove for half an hour dutifully charring the aubergines, when a hot oven will see to rendering them soft and tender. I know you don't get the smoky savour, but, just as bacon and hams come smoked and unsmoked, so too do aubergines. Yogurt takes the place of tahini, making for a gentler and creamier dip. The ideal is half 0%-fat and half full-fat (natural) yogurt, at the risk of being pernickety. Like so much Middle Eastern food, this is a great dish to serve at ambient temperature or newly cooled as well as hot – good finger-food for an alfresco lunch.

Serves 6

FOR THE CHICKEN
2 lemons
150ml extra virgin olive oil
3 garlic cloves, peeled and crushed to a paste
1 red onion, peeled and finely chopped
2 heaped teaspoons za'atar
2 cinnamon sticks, broken in half
1.8–2kg free-range chicken thighs and drumsticks
sea salt, black pepper
50g pinenuts

FOR THE AUBERGINE YOGURT
2 aubergines (500–700g total)
1 small or ½ garlic clove, crushed to a paste
150g natural Greek yogurt
1 tablespoon extra virgin olive oil, plus an extra couple
  of tablespoons to serve
1 tablespoon lemon juice
2 tablespoons finely chopped flat-leaf parsley or coriander,
  plus extra to serve

Slice one of the lemons, discarding the ends, and juice the other. Combine the lemon juice and olive oil, garlic, onion, za'atar, cinnamon and sliced lemon in a large bowl. Add the chicken pieces to the bowl and coat with the marinade. Cover and chill for several hours.

Preheat the oven to 200°C fan/220°C/gas mark 7, prick the aubergines all over with a skewer to stop them bursting and roast for 45–60 minutes until wrinkled, blackened and soft, then leave to cool. Cut off the ends, peel off the skin, halve lengthways and coarsely chop. Place the flesh in a sieve and press out the excess liquid using the back of a large spoon. Briefly whizz to a coarse purée with the garlic and some salt in a food processor. Transfer to a bowl and stir in the yogurt, then the olive oil and lemon juice. Stir in the parsley or coriander, drizzle over the extra oil and scatter over some more herbs. Set aside.

Reheat the oven to 200°C fan/220°C/gas mark 7 if you turned it off. Season the chicken pieces and arrange, skin-side up, in a single layer in two roasting pans, drizzle over the marinade and tuck the lemon slices between them. Roast for 35 minutes until golden, scattering over the pine nuts after 15 minutes. Skim off the excess fat and serve with the yogurt sauce.

SOURCE OF VITS D, B3, PHOSPHOROUS, SELENIUM
Energy 691 Kcal | Fat 49g | Sat fat 11.3g | Carbs 7.5g | Sugar 5.8g | Protein 52.9g | Salt 0.5g

CHICKEN TIKKA MASALA

This marinade is one of yogurt's claims to fame in a sauce, and provides the body for the spicy yellow crust on chicken tikka that we know and love so well.

Serves 4

FOR THE CHICKEN
4 tablespoons groundnut or rapeseed oil
1 onion, peeled and finely chopped
3 garlic cloves, peeled and crushed to a paste
5cm piece of fresh ginger, peeled and grated
1 teaspoon yellow mustard seeds
½ teaspoon ground cumin
1 teaspoon garam masala
½ teaspoon cayenne pepper
100g tomato purée
sea salt
150ml natural yogurt
600g skinless free-range chicken thigh fillets, or 4 chicken breasts

FOR THE HERB DRIZZLE
10g each coriander, mint and basil leaves
4 tablespoons extra virgin olive oil
1-2 teaspoons lemon or lime juice
½ teaspoon chopped medium–hot green chilli
½ teaspoon chopped shallot
sea salt

TO SERVE
4 large or 8 small warm wraps
½ thinly sliced cucumber
4 tablespoons (100g) soured cream
2 spring onions, trimmed and sliced
coarsely chopped coriander

To make the marinade, heat a couple of tablespoons of the oil in a large frying pan over a medium heat, add the onion and fry for 3–4 minutes until softened and starting to colour, stirring frequently. Add the garlic and ginger and cook for a minute or so longer. Now stir in the spices and cook briefly for about a minute until fragrant. Stir in the tomato purée, season with salt and cook for a further minute or so. Scrape into a food processor and whizz to a paste with the yogurt, then leave to cool.

Open out the chicken thighs and gently bash until evenly thick between sheets of clingfilm using a rolling pin. For breasts, cut out the white tendon, if visible, from the underside of each one. Place the chicken in a large bowl, coat with the marinade, cover and chill for a couple of hours. Meanwhile, place all the ingredients for the herb drizzle in a food processor and whizz to a thick green sauce. Cover and chill until required.

Heat the grill on medium–high, or set the grill pan slightly away from the heat to avoid flare-ups. You will either need a grill pan or an extra-large roasting pan. The chicken should be lightly coated in the marinade, so scrape off any excess, season and drizzle the remaining oil over either side. Grill for 6–8 minutes on each side until blackened at the tips and firm when pressed. Serve with all the little sides for assembling wraps, with the herb drizzle, if wished. You may want to slice the chicken first.

SOURCE OF VIT B12, PHOSPHOROUS
Energy 513 Kcal | Fat 26.1g | Sat fat 7.9g | Carbs 35g | Sugar 6g | Protein33.1g | Salt 0.6g

GUINEA FOWL WITH CHILLI-AVO SAUCE

This relaxed all-in-one is dished up with a guacamole-style sauce, with lots of coriander and lightly spiced with chilli; just the ticket on a cold wintery evening.

Serves 4

FOR THE GUINEA FOWL
3 medium carrots, trimmed, peeled and thickly sliced
2 parsnips, trimmed, peeled and thickly sliced
2 leeks, trimmed and thickly sliced
200g cauliflower florets (3–4cm)
1 red onion, peeled and cut into slim wedges
8 garlic cloves, unpeeled
1 medium–hot red chilli
2 bay leaves
4 tablespoons extra virgin olive oil
sea salt, black pepper
1 × 1.2–1.5kg guinea fowl, untrussed

FOR THE CHILLI-AVO SAUCE
large handful of coriander leaves
large handful of mint leaves
2 spring onions, trimmed and chopped
2 avocados, halved and stoned
100g ricotta, drained
2 tablespoons lime juice

Preheat the oven to 190°C fan/210°C/gas mark 6½. Combine the carrots, parsnips, leeks, cauliflower, onion, garlic, chilli and bay leaves in a roasting pan that will hold the guinea fowl with room to spare around the outside for the veg. Toss with 3 tablespoons of the olive oil and some seasoning. Nestle the guinea fowl in the centre (don't worry about a few veg underneath), drizzle the remaining tablespoon of oil over the bird, season it and roast for 45 minutes, stirring the vegetables surrounding the bird halfway through.

In the meantime, finely chop the herbs and spring onions in a food processor. Scoop the avocado flesh into the bowl and whizz again, then add the ricotta and whizz until creamy and smooth before adding the lime juice and seasoning with a little salt. Transfer to a small serving bowl. If making in advance, cover and chill.

Transfer the guinea fowl to a warm plate and leave to rest for 20 minutes. Give the vegetables a stir and continue to cook until really golden while the bird is resting and being carved. Discarding the seeds, scrape out the inside of the chilli, finely chop the flesh and stir half of this into the sauce, then taste and add more chilli if you like it hotter. Carve the guinea fowl and serve with the vegetables and the sauce. You can squeeze the garlic from its casing as you eat.

SOURCE OF VITS A, B3
Energy 638 Kcal | Fat 36.6g | Sat fat 5.7g | Carbs 21g | Sugar 12.8g | Protein 50.1g | Salt 0.4g

TURKISH CHICKEN STEW WITH SUMAC YOGURT

With a mass of fresh herbs, orange juice and asparagus, this is light and lively, with a little in the way of luxury provided by a dollop of yogurt relish, which is scented with sumac and its restrained hint of lemon.

Serves 4

FOR THE CHICKEN STEW
sea salt, black pepper
1.4–1.6kg free-range chicken thighs and drumsticks
2 tablespoons extra virgin olive oil
3 leeks, trimmed and thickly sliced
3 garlic cloves, peeled and thinly sliced
1 cinnamon stick
1 teaspoon ground allspice
2 thick strips of orange zest, removed with a potato peeler
1 medium–hot red chilli
150ml smooth orange juice
150ml white wine
300g fine asparagus, trimmed, and cut into 2–3cm lengths
large handful of coarsely chopped mint
large handful of coarsely chopped coriander, plus extra for scattering

FOR THE SUMAC YOGURT
150g low-fat Greek yogurt
50g soured cream
1 heaped teaspoon sumac
squeeze of lemon juice

Preheat the oven to 150°C fan/170°C/gas mark 3½. Heat a large cast-iron casserole over a medium heat, and season the chicken pieces on each side. Add a tablespoon of oil to the pan and colour the chicken on both sides, working in batches, removing the pieces to a bowl as you go. Tip out the fat, add the remaining tablespoon of oil, turn the heat down a little and fry the leeks for several minutes until glossy and starting to colour, stirring frequently. Stir in the garlic, cinnamon, allspice, orange zest and chilli and fry for about 1 minute longer until fragrant. Add the orange juice and wine, and nestle the chicken pieces into the sauce, which will half-cover it. Bring the liquid to a simmer, cover and cook in the oven for 1 hour or until the chicken is tender, turning the pieces halfway through.

Combine the ingredients for the sumac yogurt with a little salt in a small bowl.

Transfer the chicken to a large bowl and cover with foil. Skim any excess fat off the cooking juices and discard the orange zest, chilli and cinnamon stick. Bring the liquid to the boil, add the asparagus and simmer vigorously for 7–10 minutes until tender and the sauce has enriched a little, then taste for salt. Stir the mint and coriander into the sauce, and serve this ladled over the chicken pieces, dolloped with the sumac yogurt and scattered with more coriander.

SOURCE OF VIT B3
Energy 568 Kcal | Fat 37.7g | Sat fat 12.7g | Carbs 11.3g | Sugar 10g | Protein 37.5g | Salt 0.4g

ROAST SEABASS WITH
SOURED CREAM AND CAPERS

I love this combination of soured cream and yogurt, as in the previous recipe, as you get the best of both worlds; it is healthy as well as discreetly rich. And the flavourings pay homage to tartare sauce, all those lovely little bursts of flavour that go so well with fish.

The milky seabass with the crispy ham and lively piquancy of the artichokes are such a treat on their own, it seems a shame to dilute things with any further veg. You can always follow up with a salad.

Serves 4

FOR THE SOURED CREAM AND CAPER SAUCE
30g soured cream
100g low-fat Greek yogurt
1 tablespoon small capers, rinsed and finely chopped
1 tablespoon gherkins, rinsed and finely chopped
1 heaped tablespoon finely chopped flat-leaf parsley, plus a little extra, coarsely
  chopped to serve

FOR THE FISH
2 tablespoons extra virgin olive oil
4 × 125–150g seabass fillets
sea salt, black pepper
150g artichoke hearts in oil, e.g. Saclà, cut into thin segments and drained on kitchen
  paper
4–6 slices Parma or other air-dried ham, halved lengthways
1 lemon, sliced, ends discarded

Combine all the ingredients for the sauce in a small bowl and set aside, or chill if making in advance.

Preheat the oven to 220°C fan/240°C/gas mark 9. Drizzle a little oil over the base of a roasting pan large enough to hold the seabass fillets in a single layer, with a little space in between. Heat a large non-stick frying pan over a high heat, score the skin of the seabass fillets diagonally at 3–4cm intervals, brush either side with oil and season. Sear the skin for 1–2 minutes until golden, then arrange them, skin-side up, in the roasting pan.

Scatter the artichoke hearts between and over the fish, piling the slivers of ham here and there in between. Splash over a little oil and roast for 10 minutes. Serve scattered with parsley, accompanied by the sauce and the lemon slices.

HIGH IN VIT B12, PHOSPHOROUS
Energy 270 Kcal | Fat 12.3g | Sat fat 2.9g | Carbs 3.2g | Sugar 3.2g | Protein 34.7g | Salt 1g

LF PRAWN AND TAMARIND CURRY WITH CHUNKY CUCUMBER RAITA

Tamarind sharpens this simple and lively tomato sauce, laced with ginger, garlic and mint. Of all the raitas, cucumber does it best; you want something really cooling to dampen the fire of all those chillies and spice. This chunky take on it serves as a salad instead of a sauce. I'd ladle it over some skinny noodles or plain rice.

Serves 4

FOR THE CURRY
25g tamarind block, broken up
4 tablespoons boiling water
4 tablespoons vegetable oil
3 shallots, peeled and finely chopped
1 tablespoon finely chopped fresh ginger
3 garlic cloves, peeled and finely chopped
400g can chopped tomatoes
1 tablespoon Thai fish sauce
1½ teaspoons caster sugar
¼ teaspoon cayenne pepper
sea salt
400g raw peeled king prawns
handful of small mint leaves
1 medium–hot red chilli, seeds discarded and cut into thin rings
noodles or rice, to serve

Preheat the oven to 200°C fan/220°C/gas mark 7. Cover the tamarind pulp with the boiling water in a small bowl and set aside for 20 minutes, stirring occasionally as it softens. Heat 2 tablespoons of oil in a medium saucepan over a medium heat and fry the shallots, ginger and garlic for a few minutes until softened, stirring frequently. Press the tamarind purée through a sieve into the pan, discarding the fibres. Add the tomatoes, fish sauce, sugar, cayenne and a little salt, bring to the boil and simmer over a low heat for about 20 minutes until you have a rich, well-reduced sauce. This can be made in advance.

Stir the prawns, half the mint leaves and the chilli rings into the sauce and transfer to a roasting or gratin dish (about 30 × 20cm) that holds the curry in a shallow layer. Drizzle over the remaining 2 tablespoons of oil and roast for 10 minutes, then scatter over a few more mint leaves. Serve with rice or noodles and the raita.

HIGH IN VIT B12
Energy 453 Kcal | Fat 12.4g | Sat fat 1.4g | Carbs 60.3g | Sugar 5g | Protein 24.1g | Salt 1.2g

FOR THE CUCUMBER RAITA
1 cucumber, ends discarded, peeled and finely sliced
sea salt
250g natural Greek yogurt
large pinch of caster sugar
¼ teaspoon cumin seeds (or ground cumin)
paprika (optional)

Place the cucumber slices in a bowl, toss with a liberal sprinkling of salt and set aside for 30 minutes to draw out the juices. Rinse the cucumber in a sieve and pat dry.

Mix the yogurt with the sugar and a little salt in a bowl, then fold in the cucumber. Transfer to a clean serving bowl, coarsely grind the cumin seeds in a pestle and mortar and scatter over, and if you like a little paprika. If making it in advance, cover and chill, give it a stir before serving and then sprinkle over the spice.

(per 136g serving) Energy 92 Kcal | Fat 6.5g | Sat fat 4.2g | Carbs 4.2g | Sugar 4g | Protein 4g | Salt 0.1g

VEGGIES

LF ROAST CAULIFLOWER CHEESE WITH CORIANDER

Ahh, cauliflower cheese, a dish to admire but one that doesn't sit comfortably in the healthy remit of things, when it involves lashings of white sauce. There is something about the lively bitterness of cauliflower with the comfort of melting cheese that is so very good, and this way of roasting the cauli and then drizzling over some baked Camembert endeavours to capture that pleasure.

The temperature here is a little higher than you might normally bake a Camembert (e.g. 150°C fan/170°C/gas mark 3 for 25 minutes), but at worst it might get a little excited and start oozing from the box. Nothing too drastic.

Serves 4

500g cauliflower florets (2–3cm)
1 red onion, peeled, halved and sliced across
3 tablespoons extra virgin olive oil
1 tablespoon lemon juice
sea salt
1 heaped teaspoon coriander seeds, coarsely ground
250g Camembert in its wooden box
2 large handfuls rocket or watercress

Preheat the oven to 190°C fan/210°C/gas mark 6½. Arrange the cauliflower in a single layer in a large roasting pan then mix in the onion separating out the strands. Drizzle over the olive oil and lemon juice and stir to coat, then season with salt and scatter over the coriander seeds. Roast for 30 minutes until golden at the edges, stirring halfway through.

Having put the cauliflower in, remove any waxed paper surrounding the cheese, and place it back in its box. Now tie a piece of string around the side of the box to secure it. Bake for 15–20 minutes.

Spoon the cauliflower onto plates. Take the Camembert to the table, remove the wooden lid and then, using a spoon, carefully peel back the surface rind. Drizzle the molten cheese over the cauliflower and serve with a pile of rocket or watercress leaves.

HIGH IN VIT C, FOLATE | SOURCE OF VITS K, B6
Energy 324 Kcal | Fat 23.9g | Sat fat 10.4g | Carbs 6.5g | Sugar 5.1g | Protein 18.7g | Salt 1g

LF CORN COBS WITH LIME AND STAR ANISE BUTTER

Sweetcorn is a natural sop for melted butter; having nibbled off the kernels, the core that is left is made for the purpose of soaking up whatever juices are left. Goat's butter is enticing stuff, if rare, and has a flavour reminiscent of the curd, but not overly strong. It is clean and sweet, and makes a worthy surrogate with this vegetable. And a little lime in with the butter goes some way to balancing out the corn's sweetness.

Serves 3 as a light dish

50g salted butter (ideally goat's)
2 star anise
finely grated zest of 1 lime, plus 1 tablespoon juice
6 sweetcorn cobettes (half cobs)
1 tablespoon finely chopped medium–hot red chilli
2 tablespoons finely chopped coriander

Gently melt the butter in small saucepan with the star anise and lime zest and set aside to infuse. Bring a large pan of water to the boil, add the corn and cook for 5–8 minutes until tender, then drain into a colander and leave for a few minutes to steam-dry.

Gently reheat the butter, then add the lime juice, chilli and coriander. Add the corn and stir to coat with the butter, then transfer to a serving plate and drizzle over the remainder.

Griddled You can also griddle the cooked cobs: while they are steam-drying, heat a ridged griddle pan over a high heat and grill the corn for a few minutes either side until a few kernels blacken.

Energy 244 Kcal | Fat 16g | Sat fat 8.9g | Carbs 19.2g | Sugar 2.6g | Protein 4.5g | Salt 0.3g

LF SAFFRON CAULIFLOWER RICE

The idea of a low-carb stand-in for rice or couscous made with cauliflower or broccoli is inspired, and the shops have been quick to catch on, but to my way of thinking the fresher the better, so here is one to whizz up at home. This pilaf has an exotic edge – you could dish it up with a spicy ragout or curry, or simply eat it with a dollop of yogurt. Another ruse would be to stir in some cooked green lentils.

Serves 4

400g cauliflower florets
sea salt
about 20 saffron filaments, ground and blended with 1 teaspoon boiling water
25g toasted flaked almonds
50g raisins
4 tablespoons coarsely chopped coriander
15g salted butter
ewe's milk or other creamy Greek-style yogurt, to serve (optional)

Trim any excess stalk from the florets, then whizz them in batches in a food processor until they resemble grains of rice. Spread these in a thick layer over the base of a steamer in a large saucepan with a little simmering water below, and season with salt. Cover and cook for 7 minutes until tender, then drizzle the saffron liquid over the cauliflower so that just a few patches are stained, cover and leave for 5 minutes.

Carefully tip the rice into a serving bowl, mix in the almonds, raisins and coriander and dot with the butter. You may like to serve this with a dollop of a creamy yogurt too.

HIGH IN VIT C | SOURCE OF VIT B6, FOLATE, POTASSIUM, MANGANESE
Energy 144 Kcal | Fat 7.6g | Sat fat 2.4g | Carbs 11.8g | Sugar 11.1g | Protein 5.8g | Salt 0.1g

LF ROAST ASPARAGUS WITH MARCONA ALMONDS

Asparagus has ever lent itself to melted butter, and there are few better ways of enjoying it steamed or blanched, so this fusion with olive oil scented with freshly ground nutmeg and saffron stays true to that union. Try to find the round Spanish Marcona almonds, which are especially good, to complete the medley.

Serves 2

500g thick asparagus
pinch of saffron filaments (about 20), ground
1 tablespoon white wine
25g unsalted butter
1 tablespoon extra virgin olive oil
½ teaspoon freshly ground nutmeg
pinch of cayenne pepper
sea salt
1 tablespoon roasted Marcona almonds, finely chopped
1 tablespoon finely chopped flat-leaf parsley
wholemeal or plain warm flatbreads, to serve

Preheat the oven to 220°C fan/240°C/gas mark 9. Trim the asparagus spears where they become visibly woody and the deep green starts to pale. Blend the saffron with the white wine, then combine this with the butter, olive oil, nutmeg, cayenne and some salt in a small saucepan and gently heat to melt the butter. Drizzle this over the vegetables in a large roasting pan and toss to coat them. Roast for 20 minutes until lightly coloured.

Transfer to a serving dish, with any juices, and scatter over the nuts and parsley. Accompany with flatbreads for mopping.

HIGH IN FOLATE | SOURCE OF VITS K, C
Energy 277 Kcal | Fat 22.5g | Sat fat 8.3g | Carbs 5.7g | Sugar 5.1g | Protein 9g | Salt 0.2g

PEA AND PARMESAN FRITTERS

Fritters and omelettes are one and the same thing here – small, thin and crisp around the outside. My fancy goes to a few green leaves to spar with the peas and Parmesan, good 'to go' inside a buttered roll.

Serves 4/Makes approx. 8

FOR THE FRITTERS
2 tablespoons extra virgin olive oil, plus extra for frying
sea salt, black pepper
½ teaspoon caster sugar
200g fresh shelled peas
4 medium free-range eggs
1 tablespoon lemon juice
75g Parmesan, freshly grated
4 tablespoons coarsely chopped flat-leaf parsley, plus extra (optional), to serve

ROCKET SALAD (OPTIONAL)
large handful of rocket leaves
1 tablespoon extra virgin olive oil
squeeze of lemon juice
handful of Parmesan shavings

Put the 2 tablespoons of olive oil in a medium saucepan with 3 tablespoons of water, ½ teaspoon of salt and the sugar. Bring this to a simmer over a high heat, add the peas and cook, tossing occasionally, for about 3 minutes until just tender, then drain.

Whisk the eggs in a large bowl with the lemon juice and some seasoning, then fold in the Parmesan, peas and parsley. You can do this a short time in advance.

Heat a large non-stick frying pan over a high heat, add about a teaspoon of oil, then drop tablespoons of the mixture into the pan, spreading them out into omelettes 10cm in diameter. Cook for about 1 minute each side until really golden. You will need to do this in batches, draining them on a double thickness of kitchen paper as you go, and adding more oil to the pan as necessary.

If serving with a salad, toss the rocket leaves with enough olive oil to coat them in a bowl, then season with a squeeze of lemon juice and a pinch of salt. Divide the fritters between four plates, pile the salad on top, scatter over a few Parmesan shavings and drizzle over a little more oil. Alternatively, just scatter the fritters with a little more parsley to serve.

HIGH IN VITS K, C, B1, B12, FOLATE, PHOSPHOROUS | SOURCE OF VIT A, FIBRE, CALCIUM, IRON, ZINC, IODINE Energy 239 Kcal | Fat 16.2g | Sat fat 5.9g | Carbs 6.4g | Sugar 2g | Protein 15.2g | Salt 0.5g

AUBERGINE WITH TOASTED GOAT'S CHEESE

Thick slices of roast aubergine with melting goat's cheese lap up this pesto made with rocket and hazelnuts. This makes a great veggie option and will serve as a main course, but equally it will stand in as part of a mezze line-up, in which case it will do for six to twelve. This is a little more pesto than is needed, but it has lots of uses thereafter.

Serves 4

FOR THE AUBERGINE
3–4 medium aubergines, ends discarded and sliced 2–3cm thick
2 tablespoons extra virgin olive oil
200–225g semi-mature goat's cheese log (approx. 5cm in diameter), e.g. Kidderton Ash, ends removed and sliced 1cm thick
sea salt, black pepper

FOR THE ROCKET PESTO
3 tablespoons extra virgin olive oil
25g rocket
25g watercress, plus a handful of sprigs to serve
½ garlic clove, peeled
20g toasted hazelnuts
1 teaspoon balsamic vinegar, plus extra to serve
squeeze of lemon juice

Preheat the oven to 190°C fan/210°C/gas mark 6½. Select about 12 slices of aubergine from the thickest section – they need to be larger than the goat's cheese slices and will also shrink slightly on roasting. Lay these out on a large baking sheet, brush with oil on both sides and very lightly season the top. Roast for 20 minutes, then turn them and cook for a further 15–20 minutes until lightly golden.

In the meantime, put all the ingredients for the pesto in a food processor, add a little seasoning and whizz to a purée.

Remove the aubergine from the oven and heat the grill. Lay a slice of goat's cheese on each aubergine slice, and drop about ½ teaspoon of pesto in the centre. Pop under the grill for 1–3 minutes until the cheese just softens, without turning runny. Serve with a few watercress sprigs, and a drizzle of olive oil and balsamic vinegar.

TIP: For an even nuttier version, replace the olive oil with 3 tablespoons hazelnut oil, and drizzle a little more over the dish at the end.

Energy 272 Kcal | Fat 22.3g | Sat fat 10.3g | Carbs 3.8g | Sugar 3.4g | Protein 12g | Salt 0.8g

LF BUTTERNUT AND TALEGGIO POT ROAST

Taleggio is a supple and tender semi-soft blue cheese from Lombardy in Italy, with a smooth pinkish washed rind and savour of sweet hay or fruits. Like Roquefort, it is traditionally matured in caves, which provide air currents that give rise to the moulds and ferments that afford its character. It melts to the texture of liquid silk, which has not been lost on the Italians who frequently serve it on a bed of polenta.

This is at its most luxurious with a few croutons thrown over, but equally the small pool of rich sweet juices will serve to coat some large pasta shells or quills.

Serves 4

FOR THE CROUTONS
2 slices day-old white bread (excluding crusts), cut into 1cm dice
2 tablespoons extra virgin olive oil
1 heaped teaspoon thyme leaves

FOR THE POT ROAST
1kg butternut squash
4 tablespoons extra virgin olive oil
sea salt, black pepper
2 leeks, trimmed and diagonally sliced
3 garlic cloves, peeled and thinly sliced
250g cherry tomatoes
1 tablespoon balsamic vinegar
100g Taleggio, rind removed and diced

Preheat the oven to 180°C fan/200°C/gas mark 6. For the croutons, toss the bread in a bowl with the olive oil and thyme. Spread the croutons out on a baking sheet and bake for 12–15 minutes until golden. Leave to cool.

At the same time, halve the butternut squash across, cut off the skin and slice into wedges 5–7cm long, scooping out the seeds from the bulb. Heat a couple of tablespoons of the oil in a large ovenproof casserole over a high heat, add the butternut, season and fry until lightly golden – two out of three sides will do. Transfer this to a bowl. Add another tablespoon of oil to the pan, then add the leeks, season and colour these also, stirring frequently and adding the garlic just before the end. Remove the pan from the heat, then stir the butternut back in, scatter over the tomatoes, drizzle over a little more oil and the vinegar, cover and cook in the oven for 30 minutes.

Scatter over the cheese, cover and set aside for 2 minutes until it starts to melt, then serve sprinkled with the croutons.

HIGH IN VIT A | SOURCE OF VIT C, FOLATE
Energy 399 Kcal | Fat 25.7g | Sat fat 7.7g | Carbs 27.3g | Sugar 14.1g | Protein 10.2g | Salt 1.2g

LF ABONDANCE AND ALMOND PEPPER RAREBITS

Marcona almonds take the place of bread in this rarebit mix, and Abondance stands in for cheddar. I fell for this mountain cheese from the French Haute-Savoie years ago, so it is great to see it travelling further afield and widely available in many supermarkets. Made from unpasteurised cow's milk, it has the same pleasingly supple texture of other mountain cheeses of that ilk, such as Beaufort. It melts beautifully and is both more understated and elegant than gruyère, with a gentle fragrance that hints at fruit and flowers, and hazelnuts.

Serves 6

6 red and yellow peppers, stalks trimmed, halved through the stalk,
  and seeds discarded
3 tablespoons extra virgin olive oil
sea salt, black pepper
1 tablespoon lemon thyme leaves or finely chopped marjoram
300g cocktail tomatoes, coarsely diced
50g roasted Marcona almonds
120g Abondance, cut up
1 teaspoon Dijon mustard
1 teaspoon Worcestershire sauce
1 tablespoon gin

Preheat the oven to 200°C fan/220°C/gas mark 7. Arrange the peppers in a roasting pan, drizzle over 2 tablespoons of the oil, season and toss to coat, then turn, cupped-side up, and scatter over the thyme or marjoram. Roast for 20 minutes, then fill with the tomatoes, drizzle over the remaining oil, season with a little salt and roast for a further 20 minutes.

In the meantime, whizz the almonds to a coarse powder in a food processor. Now add the cheese, mustard, Worcestershire sauce and gin and continue to whizz to a paste. This can also be made well in advance, then covered and chilled.

Dot the rarebit mixture over the peppers (a little over a heaped teaspoon for each one) and return to the oven for 10–15 minutes until golden. Serve straight away.

HIGH IN VITS A, C | SOURCE OF VITS E, B6
Energy 249 Kcal | Fat 17.9g | Sat fat 5.7g | Carbs 10.1g | Sugar 9.3g | Protein 8.9g | Salt 0.5g

ROAST BEETROOT WITH TOASTED CROTTINS

Roasting beetroot in this fashion is a great start for any salad; the oily roasted skins enhance their charm hugely, and it's about as quick and easy a method as you'll find. It's a tempting salad basic that you can dress up endlessly with some grains or chopped nuts. On this occasion it is dished up with some semi-mature goat's cheese, known in France as *crottins*, baked until soft and gooey, for eating with thick slices of a hearty country bread.

Serves 6

600g beetroot (the size of a large plum)
4 tablespoons extra virgin olive oil
3 teaspoons thyme leaves
sea salt, black pepper
2 teaspoons balsamic vinegar
1 tablespoon snipped chives
1 shallot, peeled and finely chopped
2 semi-mature goat's cheeses, e.g. Crottin de Chavignol or similar

Preheat the oven to 200°C fan/220°C/gas mark 7, and trim any beetroot stalks and roots. Pour a little of the olive oil into the palm of your hand, rub them together and then lightly coat the beetroot. Arrange them in a small baking dish, splash over a little more oil, scatter over half the thyme and season. Roast for 40 minutes, then leave to cool.

About 20 minutes before eating, preheat the oven to 200°C fan/220°C/gas mark 7. Trim the bottoms of the beetroot and cut them into wedges. Arrange these on a plate, drizzle over a few tablespoons of the oil and the vinegar and scatter with the chives, shallot and a little salt.

Place the goat's cheeses in a shallow ovenproof dish, scatter over the remaining thyme leaves and trickle over a little oil. Toast for 10–12 minutes until golden and crusty at the edges. The cheese should retain its shape while being soft and melted inside. Serve with the beetroot salad.

HIGH IN FOLATE | SOURCE OF MANGANESE
Energy 243 Kcal | Fat 18.3g | Sat fat 8.5g | Carbs 8g | Sugar 7.2g | Protein 10.5g | Salt 0.8g

LF HALLOUMI-HARISSA ROAST VEG

A jazzy way of dressing up those suppertime roast veg, which are a staple in our house, not least because they make for choice grazing the next day. You can vary the cheese, though a decent hallmoui made with ewe's and goat's milk and fresh mint has a delicate creamy Mediterranean flavour that fits nicely with roast veg. But any melting cheese is a goer.

Serves 6

3 medium aubergines, end of stalks trimmed, halved lengthways
3 medium courgettes, end of stalks trimmed, halved lengthways
3–4 tablespoons extra virgin olive oil
sea salt, black pepper
300g cherry tomatoes, halved
4 spring onions, trimmed and thinly sliced
1 tablespoon harissa
150g halloumi, coarsely grated
coarsely chopped flat-leaf parsley, to serve

Preheat the oven to 220°C fan/240°C/gas mark 9. Brush the aubergine and courgette halves on each side with some of the oil, season the cut side and place this face down on a couple of non-stick baking sheets. Roast for 15 minutes, then turn over and roast for a further 15 minutes. In the meantime, combine the tomatoes and spring onions.

Spread the harissa in a thin layer over the cut surface of the vegetables, then scatter over the cheese. Toss the tomatoes and spring onions with olive oil to coat and season with a little salt, then pile on top of the roast veg. Roast for a further 15 minutes until golden and the cheese is gooey. Scatter with parsley, and eat while hot and the cheese is gooey, although they still have a certain allure when they are cold.

SOURCE OF VIT C
Energy 162 Kcal | Fat 11.6g | Sat fat 4.5g | Carbs 5.5g | Sugar 5.1g | Protein 6.8g | Salt 0.9g

BUTTERNUT CHIPS WITH DATE AND MINT QUARK

Quark has the consistency of a strained Greek yogurt, so it will stand in as labna, and it's instant, as well as negligible in fat yet high in protein. So it's a win–win. This would make a fine apero snack, although you need a fork to eat the chips, and most recently I dished it up with some barbecued teriyaki chicken thighs as an East–West garden supper.

Serves 4

1.2kg butternut squash, skin and seeds removed
3 tablespoons extra virgin olive oil
sea salt, black pepper
150g quark (for homemade see page 46)
2 Medjool dates, halved lengthways, pitted and diced
1 tablespoon finely chopped mint

Preheat the oven to 210°C fan/230°C/gas mark 7. Slice the butternut into chips the thickness of your choice – French allumette-style are ever good if a little fiddly. Scatter them over the base of a large roasting pan in a crowded single layer, drizzle over 2 tablespoons of oil, season and toss to coat. Roast for 45–55 minutes, stirring every 15 minutes until golden.

In the meantime, spread the quark over the base of small shallow dish, scatter over the dates and mint and drizzle with the remaining oil. Scoop this up with the cooked chips.

HIGH IN VIT A | SOURCE OF VITS E, C, POTASSIUM
Energy 233 Kcal | Fat 8.6g | Sat fat 1.2g | Carbs 26.8g | Sugar 15.8g | Protein 9g | Salt 0.1g

GRILLED COURGETTES AND FIGS WITH A YOGURT DRESSING

This yogurt dressing can be slathered over any combination of grilled veg; it provides a luxurious finish and welcomes herbs, garlic and all the other Med gang of flavours. You can also use low-fat Greek yogurt if preferred. Here, griddling figs brings out that jammy charm; they're perfect salad material, not too sweet or assertive, and they nestle into a pile of grilled courgettes with chameleon-like panache. Lentils or bulgar wheat would be other good additions.

Serves 6

4 courgettes, ends trimmed, cut into long thin strips
2 tablespoons extra virgin olive oil
sea salt, black pepper
6 figs, stalks trimmed, quartered
100g natural Greek yogurt
¼ teaspoon caster sugar
1 tablespoon milk (optional)
1 spring onion, trimmed and thinly sliced
a few handfuls of young spinach leaves
squeeze of lemon juice
coarsely chopped mint, to serve

Heat a ridged griddle pan over a medium heat. You will need to cook the courgette slices and fig quarters in batches. Brush as many courgette slices as will fit the griddle pan on one side with olive oil, season and grill for about 3 minutes until charred with stripes, then brush the topside with oil, turn and grill for a further 3 minutes. Remove and cook the remainder in the same fashion, then brush the fig quarters with oil and grill for about 3 minutes in total, turning them once. Leave the courgettes and figs to cool.

To make the dressing, whisk the yogurt, sugar and some seasoning in a bowl, and if necessary add the milk to thin it to the consistency of salad cream, then stir in the spring onion. You can prepare the salad to this point a couple of hours in advance, in which case cover and chill the dressing, and set the courgettes and figs aside.

Shortly before serving, toss the spinach with enough olive oil to coat it, and season with a squeeze of lemon and a pinch of salt. Mix the spinach leaves into the courgette slices and figs on a large serving plate, then spoon the yogurt dressing over and scatter with mint.

SOURCE OF VITS A, K, C, FOLATE, POTASSIUM
Energy 100 Kcal | Fat 6.2g | Sat fat 1.9g | Carbs 5.9g | Sugar 5.6g | Protein 4.2g | Salt 0.1g

LF CUMIN-ROAST CARROTS WITH OSSAU-IRATY

This salad did us proud first night back from a week away in Mallorca, having stashed a small hard sheep's cheese (similar to Ossau-Iraty) into my hand luggage, and finding that carrots were pretty much the only vegetable I had risked leaving home alone for that length of time.

Ossau-Iraty is a hard sheep's milk cheese from the Basque region that lends itself to being shaved transparently fine. It marries beautifully with Middle Eastern spices, and adds a salty savour to the sweetness of roast carrots and onions.

Serves 4

500g Chantenay carrots, stalk ends trimmed, unpeeled, scrubbed and thickly sliced diagonally
4 banana shallots, peeled and thickly sliced across
2 tablespoons extra virgin olive oil
1 tablespoon lemon juice, plus an extra squeeze
1 teaspoon ground cumin
sea salt, black pepper
handful of coarsely chopped flat-leaf parsley
30g pitted black olives, sliced
60g Ossau-Iraty, finely shaved

Preheat the oven to 190°C fan/210°C/gas mark 6½. Arrange the carrots over the base of a large roasting pan, one that will hold them in a crowded single layer. Mix in the shallots, separating out the strands as far as possible. Drizzle over the oil and the tablespoon of lemon juice and toss to coat, then scatter over the cumin and some seasoning and toss again. Roast for 30–40 minutes until lightly golden, stirring halfway through, then leave to cool.

Transfer the carrots to a serving dish and mix in the parsley and olives, season with a little more lemon juice and then carefully mix in the cheese. This is a good keeper; if you want to pop any left over into the fridge, it makes a nice surprise the next day.

HIGH IN VIT A | SOURCE OF VIT K, CALCIUM
Energy 181 Kcal | Fat 13.2g | Sat fat 5.3g | Carbs 7.9g | Sugar 7.4g | Protein 5.3g | Salt 0.8g

EGGS WITH SMOKY CAULIFLOWER AND MANCHEGO

For those who like to kickstart the weekend with something spicy, this makes a lavish brunch dish, or Friday night lead-in. The savoury hit of Manchego, made from creamy sheep's milk, is a good match for the harissa-spiked veg. A wholegrain bread fits nicely here, and I wouldn't bother to skin the tomatoes; it's all the more wholesome.

Serves 2

2 tablespoons extra virgin olive oil
3 banana shallots, peeled, halved and thinly sliced across
300g cocktail tomatoes, quartered
1 heaped teaspoon harissa
1 tablespoon sun-dried tomato paste
sea salt
300g small cauliflower florets
4 medium free-range eggs
60g Manchego, finely diced
2 tablespoons coarsely chopped coriander

Heat the olive oil in a large non-stick frying pan (e.g. 26cm) over a medium heat and fry the shallots for 6–8 minutes until golden, stirring frequently. Add the tomatoes and stir for a few minutes until they turn mushy and partially collapse. Stir in the harissa, the tomato paste and some salt. Stir in the cauliflower, cover the pan with a lid that fits as tightly as possible and cook over a low heat for 15 minutes until the cauliflower is tender, stirring halfway through.

Make four craters in the mixture and break an egg into each one, then scatter over the cheese. Cover and cook for a further 4–5 minutes until the egg is just set but the yolk remains runny. Scatter over the coriander and serve straight away.

SOURCE OF VITS C, B12, FOLATE, PHOSPHOROUS
Energy 466 Kcal | Fat 33.3g | Sat fat 10.6g | Carbs 10.8g | Sugar 10g | Protein 27.5g | Salt 0.9g

FRESH & LUXURIOUS SALADS

CACIK

This Turkish cucumber and yogurt salad mirrors tzatziki yet is subtly different with dill and garlic, and the cucumber is grated rather than diced, which I think is the best part. Dill is quite a pronounced and also acquired taste; you could just as readily use some chives in lieu, and mint is good too. That aside, cacik will happily party with any roast veg salad, pilaf, grill or roast.

On the yogurt front, a 0%-fat Greek or strained yogurt can be too austere. I would go for the full-fat, or half and half, or add a tablespoon of soured cream to enrich a 0%-fat yogurt a tad.

Serves 6

500g natural Greek or strained yogurt (see above)
1 small garlic clove, peeled and crushed to a paste
sea salt
1 cucumber, ends discarded, peeled and coarsely grated
2 heaped tablespoons finely chopped dill or chives, plus a little to serve
extra virgin olive oil, for drizzling
cayenne pepper, for dusting

Spoon the yogurt into a large bowl and mix in the garlic and a little salt. Using your hands, squeeze out as much of the liquid from the cucumber as possible, then stir this into the yogurt with the dill or chives. Transfer to a serving bowl and drizzle over some olive oil, dust with cayenne and scatter with a little dill or chives.

SOURCE OF PHOSPHOROUS, IODINE
Energy 121 Kcal | Fat 9.1g | Sat fat 5.7g | Carbs 4.5g | Sugar 4.1g | Protein 5.1g | Salt 0.1g

GREEK SALAD STACK

I wish this way of serving a Greek salad was of my own devising, but it is the inspiration of the chef at the enchanting Mallorcan hotel Petit Cala Fornells. Anything tastes good eaten in the shade of pines overlooking the Med, and this was one of those idyllic June lunches.

Back at home, given a sunny morning, warm the tomatoes on a sill or stone ledge for a couple of hours in advance of slicing them. And you want really characterful heirloom types to do the salad justice. Equally, source some barrel-aged feta for the best flavour.

Serves 2

2 beefsteak tomatoes
sea salt, black pepper
3–4 tablespoons extra virgin olive oil
1 banana shallot, peeled, halved lengthways and very finely sliced
60g feta, finely diced
40g oily pitted black olives, halved
2 teaspoons balsamic vinegar

Thinly slice the tomatoes across, and discard the end slice with the core. Now re-form each tomato on a dinner plate, seasoning every other slice and drizzling over a teaspoon of oil. Pile the shallot on top, and the feta and olives around the outside. Drizzle a couple of teaspoons of oil over the feta and olives on each plate, along with the balsamic vinegar.

SOURCE OF VIT C
Energy 293 Kcal | Fat 25.5g | Sat fat 7g | Carbs 7.4g | Sugar 7.4g | Protein 6.6g | Salt 2.3g

GAZPACHO SALAD WITH MANCHEGO AND OLIVES

All the salad ingredients that go to make a good gazpacho are present and correct here. It exudes cooling hot-weather charm, and lends itself to some fine shavings of cheese – any hard ewe's or goat's cheese, including Manchego and Ossau-Iraty. A particular treat would be the Fleur du Maquis that comes smothered with herbs from the Corsican scrub.

Serves 4

1 small cucumber, ends discarded, peeled, halved and finely sliced
250g cocktail tomatoes on the vine, quartered
¼ red onion, finely chopped
1 teaspoon finely chopped medium–hot red chilli
1 small garlic clove or ½ large clove, peeled and finely chopped
4 tablespoons coarsely chopped flat-leaf parsley
4 tablespoons extra virgin olive oil
1 tablespoon sherry vinegar or red wine vinegar
sea salt, black pepper
70g Manchego or hard sheep's or goat's cheese, finely shaved
50g pitted black olives

Combine the cucumber, tomatoes, onion, chilli, garlic and parsley in a serving bowl. Just before serving, dress with the olive oil and the vinegar, and season generously. Mix in the cheese and olives and serve straight away.

HIGH IN VIT K | SOURCE OF VITS A, C, B12, CALCIUM
Energy 212 Kcal | Fat 18g | Sat fat 5.2g | Carbs 3.8g | Sugar 3.3g | Protein 7.6g | Salt 1.1g

SALAD OF ROMAINE, PEAR AND PARMESAN WITH LEMON

Parmesan is one of the finest cheeses for a salad; the most fragile slivers your knife will allow provide both delicacy and that perfumed hit. A bowl of rocket with shavings of Parmesan and a lemon-scented oil goes down on my list of all-time great convenience salads, which is mirrored here. Though, if you are thinking ahead, you could steep some olive oil with lemon zest overnight or for several days. Remove the zest with a potato peeler, and bruise it using a pestle and mortar first in order to release the essential oils.

Serves 4

2 Cos (Romaine) lettuce hearts
1 punnet mustard and cress
about 4 tablespoons extra virgin olive oil
finely grated zest of 1 lemon, plus a squeeze of juice
sea salt
1 pear, peeled, quartered, cored and thinly sliced
75g Parmesan, finely shaved

Separate out the lettuce leaves, cut off the tops and slice the remaining leafy sections away from the thick stalks, which you can discard. Combine the lettuce with half the mustard and cress in a large bowl, and toss with 3 tablespoons of olive oil, a squeeze of lemon juice and a pinch of salt, then mix in the pear and half the Parmesan. Either arrange this on a large serving dish, or share it between four plates. Scatter over the remaining Parmesan and mustard and cress, drizzle over a little more oil and scatter over the lemon zest.

SOURCE OF FOLATE
Energy 231 Kcal | Fat 15.5g | Sat fat 5g | Carbs 10.5g | Sugar 10.5g | Protein 9.4g | Salt 0.4g

FRENCH BEANS, FIGS AND FETA

Jammy figs make for a magical summer mélange with salty sheep's cheese. With a healthy portion of green beans in its midst, this salad is all you need for a light lunch.

Serves 6

400g fine green beans, stalks trimmed and halved into shorter lengths
1 tablespoon balsamic vinegar
sea salt, black pepper
5 tablespoons extra virgin olive oil
1 tablespoon finely chopped shallot
2 large handfuls of coarsely chopped flat-leaf parsley
200g fresh figs (4 or 5), stalks trimmed and cut into thin wedges
150g feta, coarsely crumbled

Bring a large pan of salted water to the boil, add the beans and cook for 3 minutes or until just tender. Drain into a colander and refresh under the cold tap. Leave to cool.

Whisk the vinegar with some seasoning in a small bowl, then whisk in the oil. Toss the beans with half the dressing in a large bowl, and mix in the shallot and half the parsley. Transfer these to a serving plate, scatter over the figs and feta and drizzle over the remaining dressing, then scatter over the rest of the parsley.

HIGH IN VIT K | SOURCE OF FOLATE
Energy 183 Kcal | Fat 14.7g | Sat fat 4.8g | Carbs 5.6g | Sugar 5g | Protein 5.7g | Salt 0.9g

GRILLED HALLOUMI WITH COS AND ALMOND SALAD

As it becomes harder to buy whole lettuces as opposed to a 'selection of leaves', Cos, or Romaine, hearts remain one of the best choices. Their upright crisp leaves belie the hot and arid conditions in which they thrive, hence the name, which is supposed to derive from the Greek island of Cos.

Serves 4

2 Cos (Romaine) lettuce hearts
2 tablespoons walnut or hazelnut oil
2 tablespoons lemon juice
sea salt, black pepper
50g roasted salted almonds, coarsely chopped
2 tablespoons extra virgin olive oil
250g halloumi, thinly sliced across into about 12 slices
plain flour for dusting
thick slices of warm pitta, or baby pittas, to serve

Discard any damaged outer leaves from the lettuce hearts, separate out the very small inner leaves, leaving them whole, and cut off and include any pale green sections from the larger leaves outside, then tear into manageable pieces. Place these in a serving bowl and toss with the nut oil, lemon juice and a little seasoning, then mix in the nuts.

Heat a tablespoon of the olive oil in a large non-stick frying pan over a medium–high heat. Dip half the halloumi slices into the flour and fry for 30–60 seconds on each side until golden, then repeat with the remainder. Serve straight away with the salad and pitta bread.

SOURCE OF FOLATE, MANGANESE
Energy 578 Kcal | Fat 30.5g | Sat fat 10.5g | Carbs 48.9g | Sugar 7.8g | Protein 23.4g | Salt 3.1g

LF SALAD OF MIMOLETTE AND CRUSHED WALNUTS

Mimolette mirrors Dutch cheeses like Edam and Gouda – orange, firm and slightly grainy – and the mature version in particular lends itself to Parmesan-like fine shavings. It's particularly good with walnuts. We have several walnut trees in our garden in Normandy, so an abundance laid out in large wooden boxes sees us through the winter months, and the ready availability of Norman Mimolette is fortuitous.

Serves 6

FOR THE SALAD
mixture of frisée and lamb's lettuce (enough for 6)
100g Mimolette, finely shaved
50g walnut pieces

FOR THE VINAIGRETTE
1 tablespoon cider vinegar
1 teaspoon Dijon mustard
1 teaspoon caster sugar
sea salt, black pepper
3 tablespoons walnut oil
4 tablespoons groundnut oil

First make the dressing. Whisk the vinegar, mustard, sugar and seasoning in a bowl, then gradually whisk in the oils until you have a light emulsified dressing.

Place the leaves in a large salad bowl and gently mix in the shaved Mimolette. Coarsely crush the walnuts using a pestle and mortar, then add 4 tablespoons of the vinaigrette and spoon the mixture over the salad.

HIGH IN VIT K | SOURCE OF VITS A, E, B12, FOLATE, CALCIUM, PHOSPHOROUS, MANGANESE
Energy 195 Kcal | Fat 18.3g | Sat fat 5.2g | Carbs 1.3g | Sugar 1.2g | Protein 5.9g | Salt 0.5g

LF AVOCADO, PARMESAN AND SALAD SPROUTS

This salad can also be turned into a carpaccio of avocado. Finely sliced or shaved food always tastes so good; simply cut the avocado into long thin strips about 5mm wide, instead of into chunks. As well as making for a light lunch or first course, this elegant ensemble can be dished up with any cold meats or grilled chicken.

Serves 4

4 small avocados, halved and stoned
2 tablespoons lemon juice
50g very finely shaved Parmesan*
2 tablespoons extra virgin olive oil
small handful of mustard and cress or salad sprouts
2 spring onions, trimmed and finely sliced

Cut the avocado into chunks (still in its skin), before scooping them out of the shell using a dessertspoon. Arrange these pieces on four side plates or a couple of dinner plates. Drizzle the lemon juice evenly over the avocado to coat it (which will stop it discolouring). Scatter over the Parmesan, drizzle over the olive oil, pile with mustard and cress or salad sprouts and then scatter over the spring onions. The salad can be prepared 30–60 minutes in advance.

*If you have a cheese slice, this will give you gossamer-fine curled shavings.

SOURCE OF VITS E, B6, FIBRE, POTASSIUM
Energy 303 Kcal | Fat 28.7g | Sat fat 7.3g | Carbs 2.2g | Sugar 0.8g | Protein 6.5g | Salt 0.3g

BEETROOT, WATERMELON AND GOAT'S CURD

As well as complementing each other's deep red hues, watermelon and beetroot respond to the same sweet–sour treatment of being dressed with a fruit vinegar. It's a combination that cries out for something salty, and medium-ripe goat's cheese is perfect.

Serves 6

400g watermelon flesh, seeds discarded
300g cooked and peeled beetroot (unvinegared),
    ends trimmed, halved and sliced
1 tablespoon fruit vinegar, e.g. fig or raspberry
sea salt
4 tablespoons extra virgin olive oil
4 tablespoons each coarsely chopped flat-leaf parsley
    and snipped chives
50g baby spinach leaves
150g medium-mature goat's cheese, coarsely crumbled
30g Brazil nuts, thinly sliced

Cut the watermelon flesh into thin slices the same size as the beetroot. Combine the beetroot and watermelon in a large salad bowl. Blend the vinegar with a little salt in a small bowl, then add the oil. You can prepare the salad to this point in advance.

Shortly before serving, pour the dressing over the beetroot and watermelon and toss, then mix in the herbs and spinach, and scatter over the cheese and nuts.

HIGH IN VIT K | SOURCE OF VIT A, FOLATE
Energy 233 Kcal | Fat 17.6g | Sat fat 6.5g | Carbs 9.7g | Sugar 9.3g | Protein 7.9g | Salt 0.6g

LF PARMA HAM, OLIVE AND MOZZARELLA COCKTAIL

Cocktail glasses filled with goodies make a star out of any salad; it's the prawn cocktail allure. Dish this up with some breadsticks or mini rolls.

Serves 2

FOR THE DRESSING
4 cherry tomatoes, finely chopped
sea salt
1 teaspoon balsamic vinegar
1 tablespoon extra virgin olive oil
1 teaspoon finely chopped shallot

FOR THE POT
2 handfuls of baby spinach or ruby chard leaves
10 pitted green olives, halved
6 baby (pearl) mozzarella balls
2 slices Parma or other air-dried ham, torn into thirds

To make the dressing, sprinkle the tomatoes with a little salt in a small bowl and set aside for 15 minutes. Add the balsamic vinegar, oil and shallot.

Half-fill two small glasses, bowls or pots with the spinach or ruby chard leaves. Scatter over the olives and the mozzarella balls. Drape the ham in piles here and there. The cocktails can be prepared a few hours in advance. Spoon over the dressing to serve.

HIGH IN VITS A, K | SOURCE OF VIT B12, FOLATE, CALCIUM, PHOSPHOROUS
Energy 227 Kcal | Fat 18.9g | Sat fat 7.9g | Carbs 1.1g | Sugar 1.1g | Protein 12.1g | Salt 2.5g

LF ASPARAGUS, MOZZARELLA AND PEASHOOTS

A mozzarella snacking habit is a wicked one to acquire, the tempation being to reach into the fridge and tear into a soft, milky white ball to fill the void of a bored five minutes. At first it is just the one little piece, and then another and another, by which time there is no point in leaving the last lonely morsel. I am of course speaking from experience – the soft skeins of a buffalo mozzarella are one of the most indulgent dairy treats.

However, as sins go, it pales in comparison to its corrupt cousin burrata, which greets you with a buttery spurt of cream when you pierce the outside shell. The first time I tried this I died and went to heaven. And it's certainly worth bearing it in mind for a special occasion.

Asparagus and peas have long had an affinity with each other, conveniently presenting themselves to gardeners at the same time of year. And pea shoots, which are delicately tinged with the scent of peas, provide another way in.

Serves 4

150g fine asparagus, trimmed weight
4 small handfuls of pea shoots
2 × 125–150g buffalo mozzarella balls, drained and torn into pieces
about 1 tablespoon extra virgin olive oil, for drizzling
a few drops of white balsamic vinegar
sea salt
1 heaped tablespoon nonpareille (small) capers, rinsed

Bring a medium pan of salted water to the boil, add the asparagus and simmer for about 3 minutes until just tender. Drain into a colander, pass under the cold tap to stop the spears cooking any further and set aside to cool.

To serve the salad, arrange the peashoots, asparagus spears and mozzarella on four plates. Drizzle over a little oil and the balsamic vinegar, and scatter over a pinch of salt and the capers.

HIGH IN VITS K, B12, FOLATE | SOURCE OF VITS A, D, B2, CALCIUM, PHOSPHOROUS, ZINC
Energy 180 Kcal | Fat 13.8g | Sat fat 8.8g | Carbs 0.8g | Sugar 0.7g | Protein 12.8g | Salt 0.6g

QUAIL EGG SALAD WITH BUTTERMILK DRESSING

Beetroot and quail eggs have a distinctly English feel to them, as does buttermilk. The latter is an underused ingredient that we tend to save for soda bread and scones, but it is light and lively, thinner than yogurt with similar appeal, and it makes a great salad dressing. This would be at home piled onto a thick slice of buttered Granary bread.

Serves 2

FOR THE DRESSING
2 tablespoons buttermilk
1 teaspoon soured cream
sea salt
1 heaped teaspoon finely chopped chives
1 teaspoon finely chopped flat-leaf parsley
1 teaspoon finely chopped basil

FOR THE POT
2 heaped tablespoons cooked beetroot (unvinegared), cut into 1cm dice
1 teaspoon balsamic vinegar
2 handfuls of lamb's lettuce, roots pinched off
12 quail eggs, boiled for 2½ minutes, shelled and halved
2 heaped teaspoons coarsely chopped roasted cashew nuts

To make the dressing, whisk the buttermilk, soured cream and a little salt in a small bowl to blend, then stir in the herbs.

Dress the beetroot with the vinegar in another small bowl, then drain off the excess.

Arrange the lamb's lettuce on a couple of plates and scatter over the beetroot. Nestle the quail eggs between the leaves and beetroot, then spoon over the dressing and scatter with the nuts. The salads can be prepared a few hours in advance.

TIP: Try sprinkling the salad with a little celery salt before eating – if buying cooked and peeled quail eggs, they may come with a sachet.

SOURCE OF VIT B2, FOLATE, PHOSPHOROUS, IRON
Energy 196 Kcal | Fat 13.3g | Sat fat 3.8g | Carbs 5.3g | Sugar 4.1g | Protein 13.1g | Salt 0.1g

CREAMY FINISHES:
ICES, CREAMS & COMFORTS

LF CHOCOLATE, PEAR AND CHILLI CAKE

Cakes are inclined to fall into an all-or-nothing scenario when it comes to dairy, either insanely rich and buttery or fiercely right on and made with grated vegetables and oil. So I wanted a truce between the warring factions, and here the sponge takes its cue from a carrot-style cake, with just a little buttery crumble scattered over. But the real treat is the chilli that spars masterfully with the chocolate, courtesy of a dribble of Tabasco. Should you want to shout about it, then the chilli syrup provides added pep.

Makes 1 × 20cm cake/Serves 10

FOR THE CAKE
3 Conference pears
170g light muscovado sugar
1 tablespoon lemon juice
170ml groundnut or vegetable oil
2 medium free-range eggs
70ml smooth orange juice
½–1 teaspoon Tabasco, depending on taste
200g plain flour
30g cocoa
2 teaspoons baking powder
50g dark chocolate chips

FOR THE CRUMBLE
50g unsalted butter, diced, plus extra for greasing the tin
80g plain flour
80g light muscovado sugar

Peel, quarter and core the pears, then thinly slice across. Toss these in a large bowl with a couple of tablespoons of the sugar and the lemon juice and set aside for 10 minutes.

In the meantime, preheat the oven to 180°C fan/200°C/gas mark 6 and butter a 20cm cake tin with sides 7cm deep and a removable base. Whisk the oil, eggs and orange juice in a large bowl with the Tabasco to taste, and any juices given out by the pears. Whisk in the remaining sugar. Sift the flour, cocoa and baking powder together and whisk into the mixture, then stir in the pears and chocolate chips. Transfer the mixture to the cake tin.

Put the ingredients for the crumble in the bowl of a food processor and whizz until the mixture resembles fine crumbs. Scatter this over the surface of the cake and bake for 50–60 minutes until golden and risen, and a knife inserted into the centre comes out clean or with no more than a smear of chocolate on it. Run a knife around the edge and leave to cool. Serve the cake with a teaspoon of the chilli syrup (below), if wished.

SOURCE OF VIT E
Energy 476 Kcal | Fat 24.8g | Sat fat 8.1g | Carbs 56.4g | Sugar 35.4g | Protein 5g | Salt 0.5g

CHILLI SYRUP (OPTIONAL)
1 medium–hot red chilli, core and seeds discarded, cut into fine 1–2cm lengths
50ml smooth orange juice
50g caster sugar

If using, put all the ingredients into a small saucepan, bring to the boil and simmer over a very low heat for 5 minutes. Transfer this to a bowl and leave to cool.

PARISIAN BLACKCURRANT CHEESECAKE

Hard not to get a deep thrill out of the glassy magenta surface of this cheesecake, which looks as though it comes from the finest pâtisserie in Paris, and is oh so simple and virtuous to boot. If you need any convincing about the merits of fat-free curd cheese, this should do it.

Makes 1 × 20cm cheesecake/Serves 8

FOR THE CRUST
50g unsalted butter
150g plain digestive biscuits

FOR THE FILLING
3 medium free-range eggs, separated
125g golden caster sugar
finely grated zest of 1 lemon
750g quark (for homemade, see page 46)
6 gelatine leaves, cut into broad strips
3 tablespoons boiling water

FOR THE GLAZE
1 gelatine leaf, cut into broad strips
3 tablespoons boiling water
100g blackcurrant jam

For the crust, gently melt the butter in a small saucepan over a low heat. Put the biscuits inside two plastic bags, one inside the other, and crush them to fine crumbs using a rolling pin. Tip them into the saucepan with the melted butter and stir to coat them, then transfer to a 20cm cake tin with sides 6–7cm deep and a removable base, and use your fingers or the bottom of a tumbler to press them into the base.

For the filling, whizz the egg yolks, sugar and lemon zest in a food processor for a couple of minutes until pale and thick. Add the quark and whizz until smooth, leave to stand for 15 minutes, then scrape down the sides of the bowl and whizz again.

While the quark is standing, soak the gelatine strips in cold water in a medium bowl for 5 minutes, then drain. Pour over the boiling water and stir to dissolve – if necessary, stand the bowl within another bowl with boiling water in it or set over a pan with a little simmering water.

Transfer the quark mixture to a large bowl. Blend 3 tablespoons with the gelatine, one at a time so that the mixtures are more or less the same temperature, then gradually stir the gelatine solution into the base. Whisk the egg whites until stiff in a large bowl using an electric whisk and then fold these, half at a time, into the quark mixture. Carefully pour this on top of the biscuit base, using the back of a large spoon as a chute so as not to disturb the crumbs, then level the surface, cover and chill overnight.

For the glaze, soak the gelatine as above. Pour over the boiling water and stir to dissolve, then blend this, a tablespoon at a time, into the jam. Pour this over the surface of the cheesecake so that the blackcurrants are evenly distributed. Cover and chill for several hours until this has set. It will keep well for several days.

SOURCE OF VIT B6, FOLATE, PHOSPHOROUS
Energy 321 Kcal | Fat 10.4g | Sat fat 5.4g | Carbs 39.7g | Sugar 29.9g | Protein 17.1g | Salt 0.6g

PISTACHIO AND CHERRY SLICE

A tender and fudgy pistachio sponge laced with cherries and made using fromage frais to replace some of the butter, therefore making it lighter than many cakes, but alluringly moist with a crisp pastry base.

Makes 16 squares

60g unsalted butter, softened, plus extra for greasing the tin
320g sheet ready-rolled all-butter puff pastry
110g golden caster sugar
2 medium free-range eggs
200g natural fromage frais
200g ground pistachio nuts
1 teaspoon baking powder, sifted
½ teaspoon ground cinnamon, sifted
100g undyed glacé cherries, halved
icing sugar for dusting

Preheat the oven to 170°C fan/190°C/gas mark 5. Butter a 23cm square brownie tin and line the base and sides with baking paper, cutting out a square from each corner so that the sides sit flat. Cut a square of puff pastry to fit the base and lay in place. Cream the butter and sugar together in a food processor, then add the eggs, one at a time, and the fromage frais. Add the ground pistachios, baking powder and cinnamon. Smooth this on top of the pastry, scatter over the cherries and bake for 30–35 minutes until golden and firm. Leave to cool.

Carefully lift the cake out of the tin using the paper sides. For a pretty striped effect, cut out strips of baking paper 4cm wide and lay these diagonally across the cake, with 4cm in between each one. Dust the cake with icing sugar and then remove the strips. Cut off a thin slice from each of the four sides, and then cut into 16 squares. The cake will keep well in an airtight container for several days.

SOURCE OF PHOSPHOROUS
Energy 249 Kcal | Fat 16.2g | Sat fat 5.9g | Carbs 20.1g | Sugar 12.9g | Protein 5.3g | Salt 0.5g

MILK CHOCOLATE MOUSSE

Quark has a delicate creamy texture, and takes care of the cream and butter that underpin chocolate mousses. Do dig out that bottle of rum from the back of the cupboard, it works wonders with the coffee.

Serves 8

FOR THE MOUSSE
200g milk chocolate, broken into pieces
100g dark chocolate (approx. 70% cocoa), broken into pieces
500g quark
4 large free-range eggs, separated
1 tablespoon dark rum or espresso

FOR THE DECORATION
coarsely grated milk chocolate
icing sugar

Gently melt the two chocolates in a bowl set over a pan with a little simmering water in it; this needs to be at room temperature, so remove from the heat and if necessary allow to cool a little. Whizz the quark and egg yolks until smooth in a food processor, then add the chocolate and whizz again. Add the rum or coffee, and transfer this to a large bowl.

Whisk the egg whites until stiff in a large bowl using an electric whisk, then fold these, half at a time, into the chocolate base, immediately transfer to a serving bowl and smooth the surface. Cover and chill for several hours. The mousse will keep well for a couple of days. Smother with a liberal coating of grated chocolate and dust with icing sugar before serving.

HIGH IN VIT B12 | SOURCE OF VIT B2, FOLATE, PHOSPHOROUS
Energy 286 Kcal | Fat 14.8g | Sat fat 8.9g | Carbs 23.4g | Sugar 23.2g | Protein 14.6g | Salt 0.3g

CRÈME BRÛLÉE

The raison d'être of a crème brûlée is the contrast of the silken cream with the fine brittle of the caramel, and when made with milk rather than cream, the custard is even more heart-stoppingly silky but a fraction as rich. This method of drizzling the caramel over the top does away with the need for a blowtorch.

Serves 6

FOR THE CUSTARD
7 medium free-range egg yolks
80g white caster sugar
1 teaspoon vanilla bean paste
600ml whole milk

FOR THE CARAMEL
125g white caster sugar

Preheat the oven to 140°C fan/160°C/gas mark 3. Whisk the egg yolks, sugar and vanilla together in a large bowl. Bring the milk to the boil in a small saucepan, whisk it onto the egg yolk mixture and pass it through a sieve into a jug. Divide between six 150ml ramekins or heatproof glass jars. Place these in a roasting dish with hot but not boiling water that comes two-thirds of the way up the sides, and bake for 1¼ hours until set. Remove the ramekins from the roasting dish and leave to cool to room temperature, then chill for several hours or overnight, uncovered.

Within a couple of hours of serving, gently heat the sugar for the caramel in a small saucepan until about half of it has liquefied and started to colour, then gently stir it. Keep a careful eye, stirring frequently until it is a clear deep gold, then remove from the heat. Drizzle a teaspoon or two of caramel over the surface of each one; it should set hard within minutes. Chill until required.

HIGH IN VIT B12 | SOURCE OF VITS B5, B7, PHOSPHOROUS, IODINE
Energy 273 Kcal | Fat 10.3g | Sat fat 4.3g | Carbs 38.5g | Sugar 38.5g | Protein 6.6g | Salt 0.1g

LF GORGONZOLA-STUFFED DATES WITH HONEY

Pudding or cheese? These little eats bridge the gap; something to end on with a shot of espresso when you don't want to go the whole hog.

Makes 10–12

10–12 Medjool dates
100g creamy Gorgonzola
1 tablespoon runny honey

Slit the dates lengthways to remove the stones. Generously fill with the Gorgonzola, and arrange on a plate. Drizzle over the honey to serve.

SOURCE OF VIT B2, FIBRE, POTASSIUM, CALCIUM, PHOSPHOROUS
(per date) Energy 83 Kcal | Fat 2.8g | Sat fat 1.7g | Carbs 11.9g | Sugar 11.9g | Protein 2.2g | Salt 0.4g

VANILLA PANNA COTTA

Greek yogurt makes for a delicate panna cotta; in keeping, it is lily white and just as silky as if it were made with cream, but so much healthier. I actively prefer this, and don't think it misses anything by eschewing the all-cream route.

Serves 4

2 gelatine leaves, cut into broad strips
3 tablespoons boiling water
450g natural Greek yogurt
75g white caster sugar
1 teaspoon vanilla bean paste
4 tablespoons kirsch or fruit vodka
100g seedless black or red grapes, halved

Place the gelatine strips in a medium bowl, cover with cold water and soak for 5 minutes, then drain. Pour the boiling water over the gelatine and stir to dissolve. Put the yogurt and sugar in a small saucepan and gently heat until the sugar dissolves, stirring constantly and taking care not to boil, then remove from the heat and stir in the vanilla bean paste.

Blend 3 tablespoons of the yogurt into the gelatine, one at a time, and then stir this back in with the rest of the yogurt. Divide the mixture between four 150ml ramekins or some other pretty non-stick moulds. Cover and chill in the fridge for several hours or overnight until set. They will keep well for several days. To serve, run a knife around the edge of each cream to loosen it, and then turn it out onto a plate. Pour a tablespoon of kirsch or fruit vodka over each cream and scatter with grapes.

Energy 276 Kcal | Fat 11.5g | Sat fat 7.6g | Carbs 27.6g | Sugar 27.2g | Protein 7.6g | Salt 0.2g

FIVE-HOUR ORANGE RICE PUD

The notion that rice, milk and sugar can be turned into this creamy pudding as a result of time and chemistry is a matter of wonder. One of the finest renditions derives from Normandy, where they are tremendously proud of their rice pudding – it is always heartening when you go to one of the big chain hypermarkets and alongside the global brand yogurts there are tubs of locally made rice pudding. But, as ever, there is nothing quite like homemade, with a thick bank of rice pudding, a creamy head of sauce and the golden skin we so prize. The orange subtly infuses the milk, and you can serve it with a dollop of jam, if you wish.

Serves 8

125g short-grain rice
125g golden caster sugar
finely grated zest of 1 orange
1.5 litres whole milk
ground cinnamon for dusting

Preheat the oven to 120°C fan/140°C/gas mark 1. Combine the rice, sugar and orange zest in a 20cm soufflé or deep 1.8-litre ovenproof dish, working them with a wooden spoon to make sure the zest is evenly distributed, then slowly blend in the milk. Dust with cinnamon and bake in the oven for 5 hours until covered with a thick deep brown skin, and the surface milk beneath has thickened into a thin buff-coloured cream. Either serve hot when it will be loose and creamy or at room temperature, or chilled when the rice will firm up and the milk thicken. It can also be rewarmed in the oven.

SOURCE OF IODINE
Energy 242 Kcal | Fat 7.5g | Sat fat 4.7g | Carbs 36.6g | Sugar 23.7g | Protein 7.2g | Salt 0.2g

RASPBERRY YOGURT ICE CREAM

Only three ingredients, but each with a leading role to play. The raspberry yogurt provides the character, the Greek yogurt a rich finish, while the golden syrup ensures a soft texture. You want a Greek-style yogurt here, which tends to be thinner than the real thing. And also a good raspberry yogurt – I'd head in the organic direction and check the label for unknowns. Serve drizzled with raspberry sauce, scattered with fresh raspberries and accompanied by some baby meringues.

Makes approx. 1 litre/Serves 8

500g tub natural Greek-style yogurt
500g tub full-fat raspberry yogurt
150g golden syrup

Blend all the ingredients together in a large bowl and freeze according to the instructions for your ice-cream maker. If not serving freshly churned, transfer the ice cream to a container, seal and freeze.

Remove from the freezer about 30 minutes in advance of serving if it has frozen solid.

Without a machine Alternatively, pour the mixture into a container, seal and freeze until softly frozen – start checking it after about 3 hours, and hourly thereafter. Scoop the ice cream into the bowl of a food processor and whizz to a slush, then return it to the freezer for a further few hours or overnight.

SOURCE OF VIT C
Energy 155 Kcal | Fat 5.9g | Sat fat 3.8g | Carbs 21.6g | Sugar 18.8g | Protein 3.8g | Salt 0.2g

FROZEN GRANOLA YOGURT SUNDAE

All manner of knickerbocker glory-type creations can be dreamt up for your yogurt ice. Children and teens especially might appreciate these.

Serves 4

2 bananas, peeled and cut up
2 tablespoons lemon curd
500ml yogurt ice cream (see above)
80g granola
100g blueberries
4 teaspoons dark runny honey

Whizz the bananas and the lemon curd to a purée in a food processor. Divide this between four knickerbocker glory or other tall glasses. Drop a couple of scoops of ice cream on top of the purée in each glass. Scatter over the granola and then the blueberries, and finally drizzle a teaspoon of honey over each one.

SOURCE OF IODINE
Energy 370 Kcal | Fat 6.9g | Sat fat 3.1g | Carbs 67.9g | Sugar 58.8g | Protein 7.9g | Salt 0.3g

PORRIDGE WITH BUTTERMILK AND CINNAMON

Given the essential role that breakfast plays in our lives, there are few better starting points than porridge. Alongside its many accolades, it is the ideal opportunity to add in the dairy of your choice: a little creamy buttermilk or sliver of butter. It doesn't necessarily have to be sweet, but if it does, there's nothing wrong with a spoon of stevia, and you could go down the half-and-half route with a little honey to counter its bitterness.

This is a pleasurable weekend ritual, with its comforting nutty fragrance and texture. Some Scottish devotees declare the coarser your oatmeal, the tastier it will be; others maintain that pinches of raw meal should be added to the porridge as it cooks for the richest variety of textures at the end. Plenty of scope for debate and early morning enterprise.

Serves 2

Method Soak 1 cup of pinhead oatmeal in 3 cups of water overnight. Transfer the contents to a small saucepan and bring to the boil over a medium heat, stirring frequently. In Shetland, this is traditionally done using a spirtle or gruel-tree (a wooden stick about 30cm long). Turn the heat down and leave it to splutter for 3–4 minutes until tender. Only add the salt towards the end, a good pinch of it, otherwise it hardens the grains. Serve the porridge with a splash of milk or buttermilk, a sprinkling of cinnamon and light muscovado sugar or a spoon of honey. A tot of whisky is not untraditional – it is the weekend, after all.

SOURCE OF CALCIUM, PHOSPHOROUS
Energy 122 Kcal | Fat 2.3g | Sat fat 0.4g | Carbs 20.7g | Sugar 5.5g | Protein 3.4g | Salt 2.9g

HONEY YOGURT ICE CREAM

We'd eat so much more ice cream if conscience wasn't at stake, and yogurt ice is a masterful pretender; its resulting texture mirrors a classic egg custard base, giving the ice cream a heavy luscious melt without the fat and guilt. The plus to homemade is authenticity; the small print on a tub of bought-in yogurt ice reveals that just about everything goes into the commercial ones except yogurt. And they are the simplest of ices to make.

Makes approx. 1 litre/Serves 8

175g white caster sugar
75g runny honey, plus extra (optional), to serve
1 teaspoon vanilla extract
900g natural yogurt

Stir the sugar, honey and vanilla into the yogurt in a large bowl, then continue to stir occasionally over the next 10 minutes until the sugar has dissolved. Freeze according to the instructions for your ice-cream maker. If not serving straight away, then spoon into a tub or attractive serving dish, cover and freeze. You can serve with an additional drizzle of honey.

Without a machine Alternatively, pour the ice cream solution into a container, seal and freeze until softly frozen – start checking it after about 3 hours, and hourly thereafter. Scoop the ice cream into a food processor and whizz to a thick slush. Return it to the container and freeze for a further few hours or overnight. If you want to serve it ice-cream parlour style, leave it to soften out of the freezer for about 20 minutes, before mounding it in scoops in a serving dish, then drizzle over a little more honey.

HIGH IN IODINE | SOURCE OF CALCIUM, PHOSPHOROUS
Energy 204 Kcal | Fat 3.4g | Sat fat 2.1g | Carbs 37.1g | Sugar 37.1g | Protein 6.3g | Salt 0.2g

GIN AND LEMON DELIGHT

I blame my teenage son and his links to the Portobello Star, with their artisanal gin distillery where he worked during his gap year, for the reason I find myself reaching for the gin bottle more and more. Portobello gin that is, which down at 'The Ginstitute' they instil with every imaginable aromatic during their sessions.

Serves 4

2 gelatine leaves, cut into broad strips
2 tablespoons gin
finely grated zest and juice of 1 lemon
250g quark (for homemade see page 46)
3 tablespoons double cream
2 medium free-range egg whites
50g white caster sugar
edible flower petals, to decorate (optional)
delicate dessert biscuits, to serve

Place the gelatine strips in a medium bowl, cover with cold water and soak for 5 minutes, then drain. Gently warm the gin and lemon juice in a small saucepan to just below boiling point, pour this over the gelatine and stir to dissolve, then leave to cool to room temperature. Whizz the quark, cream and lemon zest in a food processor until smooth, then gradually trickle in the gelatine solution through the funnel with the motor running, and transfer to a large bowl.

Whisk the egg whites until stiff in a medium bowl using an electric whisk, then sprinkle over the sugar, a tablespoon at a time, whisking well with each addition until you have a stiff, glossy meringue. Fold this into the quark base, half at a time, using a wooden spoon, then mound into six 150ml ramekins or little glasses and chill for several hours until set. Cover if keeping for longer; it will be good for several days. Decorate with edible flower petals if wished, and serve with biscuits.

SOURCE OF VIT E, PHOSPHOROUS
Energy 267 Kcal | Fat 11.6g | Sat fat 4.9g | Carbs 23.1g | Sugar 18g | Protein 13.5g | Salt 0.3g

BUCKWHEAT PANCAKES WITH SALTED BUTTER AND HONEY

Buckwheat flour is lovely stuff, seal-grey with black flecks, faintly sour, delicate and altogether more elegant than wholemeal flour. So it's a good way to up our much-needed intake of wholegrains. We are most familiar with its warm musty scent in blinis. And while we treat buckwheat as a cereal, it is actually a herb of the genus *Fagopyrum*. Its English name is beech wheat, due to the shape of the grains, which are a little like beech nuts.

These blini-style pancakes lend themselves to savoury options as well as sweet – smoked salmon and sour cream in particular.

Makes 25/Serves 6

FOR THE PANCAKES
80g plain flour
80g buckwheat flour
2 teaspoons baking powder
pinch of golden caster sugar
pinch of fine sea salt
1 medium free-range egg, separated
300ml whole milk
2 teaspoons groundnut or vegetable oil for grilling

TO SERVE
softened salted butter
honeycomb

Sift the flours and baking powder into a large bowl and then add the sugar and salt. Whisk the egg yolk and milk in another bowl until blended. Pour this mixture onto the sifted dry ingredients and whisk until smooth. Leave to stand for 10 minutes. Whisk the egg white until stiff in a medium bowl using an electric whisk and fold it into the pancake mixture.

In the meantime, heat a cast-iron frying pan or flat griddle over a lowish heat for 10 minutes until it reaches an even snug warmth. Grease the hot iron with oil using a brush, then drop tablespoons of the mixture into the pan, spaced slightly apart. Cook for 1–2 minutes until the surface pits with bubbles, then carefully turn the pancakes using a palette knife and cook for about 1 minute more until golden on the underside. You should find the first side is completely smooth, while the underside looks more like a crumpet. Remove them to a plate, smear with a little salted butter and a dollop of honeycomb, and eat while you put some more on to cook, re-oiling the pan now and again between batches as it needs it. Alternatively, if you are making them in advance, then keep them covered with foil on a plate for up to 30 minutes. They can also be reheated in an oven preheated to 160°C fan/180°C/gas mark 4. Stack them about six high, wrap in foil and heat for 20 minutes.

HIGH IN PHOSPHOROUS | SOURCE OF VIT B12, MANGANESE
Energy 214 Kcal | Fat 8.1g | Sat fat 4.3g | Carbs 29.8g | Sugar 8.9g | Protein 4.9g | Salt 0.6g

bibliography

BOOKS

The Big Fat Surprise: Why Butter, Meat and Cheese Belong in a Healthy Diet
Nina Teicholz
(Scribe, 2015)

The Cheese Room
Patricia Michelson
(Michael Joseph, 2001)

Cheesemaking and Dairying
Katie Thear
(Broad Leys Publishing, 1978, 4th edn 2006)

Cheeses of the World
Bernard Nantet, Patrick Rance, Françoise Botkine, Ninette Lyon and Jean-Claude Ribaut
(Little, Brown and Company, 1992)

Classic Cheese Cookery
Peter Graham
(Penguin, 1998)

Guide du Fromage
Pierre Androuet
(English edn, Aidan Ellis, 1983)

Human Nutrition
Catherine Geissler and Hilary Powers, eds
(Churchill Livingstone Elsevier, 12th edn, 2011)

McCance and Widdowson's The Composition of Foods
(Food Standards Agency, 2002, 6th summary edn)

Nutrition: A Lifespan Approach
Simon Langley-Evans
(Wiley-Blackwell, 2009)

On Food and Cooking: The Science and Lore of the Kitchen
Harold McGee
(HarperCollins, 1984, revised edn 1991)

The Oxford Companion to Food
Alan Davidson
(Oxford University Press, 3rd edn, 1999)

Understanding Nutrition
Eleanor Whitney and Sharon Rady Rolfes
(Wadsworth, 14th edn, 2016)

The World Encyclopedia of Cheese
Juliet Harbutt and Roz Denny
(Lorenz Books, 1998)

PRINTED PAPERS AND ARTICLES

'Lactose Intolerance', Daniel L. Swagerty, JR, MD, MPH, Anne D. Walling, MD, and Robert M. Klein, PHD, *American Family Physician*, 2002, 65(9), 1845–1851

'Calcium supplementation and bone mineral accretion in adolescent girls: an 18-month RCT with 2-year follow-up', Helen L. Lambert, Richard Eastell, Kavita Karnik, Jean M. Russell and Margo E. Barker, *American Journal Clinical Nutrition*, 2008 (87), 455–462

'Review article: lactose intolerance in clinical practice – myths and realities', M. C. E. Lomer, G. C. Parkes, J. D. Sanderson, *Alimentary Pharmacology and Therapeutics,* 2008, 27(2), 93–103

'Effects of calcium supplementation on bone density in healthy children: meta-analysis of randomised controlled trials', Tania Winzenberg, Kelly Shaw, Jayne Fryer and Graeme Jones, *British Medical Journal,* 2006, 333(7572), 775–778

'Effects of vitamin D supplementation on bone density in healthy children: systematic review and meta-analysis', Tania Winzenberg, Sandi Powell, Kelly Anne Shaw and Graeme Jones, *British Medical Journal,* 2011, 342(7791), 267

'Evaluation of the impact of ruminant trans fatty acids on human health: important aspects to consider', Katrin Kuhnt, Christian Degen and Gerhard Jahreis, *Critical Reviews of Food Science and Nutrition,* 2015, 56(12), 1964–1980

'Natural trans fat, dairy fat, partially hydrogenated oils, and cardio metabolic health: the Ludwigshafen Risk and cardiovascular Health Study', *European Heart Journal,* 2015, 595

'A reappraisal of the impact of dairy foods and milk fat on cardiovascular disease risk,' J. Bruch German, Robert A. Gibson, Ronald M. Krauss, Paul Nestel, Benoit Lamarche, Wija A. van Staveren, Jan M. Steijns, Lisette C. P. G. M. de Groot, Adam L. Lock, Frederic Destaillats, *European Journal of Nutrition,* 2009, 48(4), 191–203

'The relationship between high-fat dairy consumption and obesity, cardiovascular, and metabolic disease', Mario Kratz, Ton Baars and Stephan Guyenet, *European Journal of Nutrition*, 2013 (52), 1–24

'Saturated fatty acids and type 2 diabetes: more evidence to re-invent dietary guidelines,' Dariush Mozaffarian, *Lancet Diabetes and Endocrinology*, 2014 (2), 770–772

'Urea nitrogen salvage mechanisms and their relevance to ruminants, non-ruminants and man,' Gavin S. Stewart and Craig P. Smith, *Nutrition Research Reviews,* 2005, 18, 49–62

'Dairy product intake in children and adolescents in developed countries: trends, nutritional contribution, and a review of association with health outcomes', Daphna K. Dror and Lindsay H. Allen, *Nutrition Reviews,* 2014, 72(2), 68–81

'Is butter back? A systematic review and meta-analysis of butter consumption and risk of cardiovascular disease, diabetes, and total mortality', Laura Pimpin, Jason H. Y. Wu, Hila Haskelberg, Liana Del Gobbo, Dariush Mozaffarian, *PloS ONE*, 2016, 11(6)

REPORTS AND ONLINE PUBLICATIONS

Dietary reference values for food energy and nutrients for the United Kingdom Department of Health (HMSO, 1991)

Global Report on Diabetes (World Health Organization, 2016) www.who.int/diabetes/global-report/en

SACN Vitamin D and Health Report (Public Health England, 2016) Independent report by the Scientific Advisory Committee on Nutrition (SACN) available online: www.gov.uk/government/publications/sacn-vitamin-d-and-health-report

SACN Dietary reference values for energy (Public Health England, 2011) Independent report by the Scientific Advisory Committee on Nutrition (SACN) available online: www.gov.uk/government/publications/sacn-dietary-reference-values-for-energy

WEBSITES

British Dietetic Association
www.bda.uk.com

British Nutrition Foundation
www.bnf.org.uk

Caroline Walker Trust
www.cwt.org.uk

Change4life
www.nhs.uk/change4life

The Dairy Council
www.milk.co.uk

The Eatwell Guide
www.nhs.uk

Farming Standards
www.soilassociation.org

Lactose Intolerance
www.niddk.nih.gov

National Osteoporosis Society
www.nos.org.uk

Osteoporosis Pathways
www.pathways.nice.org.uk

SOURCE OF FIBRE at least 3g of fibre per 100g or at least 1.5g of fibre per 100kcal.

HIGH IN FIBRE at least 6g of fibre per 100g or at least 3g of fibre per 100kcal.

SOURCE OF [VITAMIN/MINERAL] at least a significant amount* as defined in the Annex to Directive 90/496/EEC or an amount provided for by derogations granted according to Article 6 of Regulation (EC) No 1925/2006 of the European Parliament and of the Council of 20 December 2006 on the addition of vitamins and minerals and of a certain other substances to foods.

HIGH IN [VITAMIN/MINERAL] at least twice the value of 'source of'.

*Note that for vitamins and minerals, 'significant amount' is based on their specified nutrient reference values (NRVs) as follows:

· 15% of the NRV supplied by 100g or 100ml of products other than beverages,

· 7.5% of the NRV supplied by 100ml of beverages or,

· 15% of the NRV per portion where there is a single portion.

VITAMIN A NRV = 800ug 15% of NRV = 120ug

VITAMIN K NRV= 75mg 15% = 11.25

CALCIUM NRV=800mg 15% = 120mg

All recipes analysed with no added salt. Salt content is due to naturally occurring sodium and salt present in ingredients.

LACTOSE INTOLERANCE

The majority of the lactose intolerant still produce some of the enzyme lactose and can deal with a small amount of lactose: some research suggests up to 12g of lactose in a single sitting (about one glass of milk). But for the recipes in this book that are marked as lactose-free (LF), the level is set at a trace of 1g per 100ml or less, which will accommodate all but extreme intolerance. Milk allergy is rarer and usually occurs in babies and it is generally due to the protein in milk rather than the sugars in milk, i.e. lactose.

NOTES

All teaspoons are rounded, or as the ingredient would naturally be spooned out of a container, unless specified as 'level' or 'heaped'.

All recipes have been tested in a fan oven, and the temperature increased by 20°C for electric ovens. Please be guided by experience of your own oven in this respect if it is likely to differ.

A single tub yogurt maker is recommended for the homemade recipes on page 43. Lakeland Electric 1-litre Yogurt Maker available from www.lakeland.co.uk.

index

A

almonds: Abondance and almond
pepper rarebits 145
grilled halloumi with cos and
almond salad 161
roast asparagus with marcona
almonds 139
anchovies: anchovy toasts with
cavolo nero 53
buttered anchovy paste 53
spinach and anchovy
bulgar-otto 115
apples: apple and goji berry
yogurt 45
broccoli and apple 120
celery, apple and Gorgonzola
soup 62
artichokes: roast seabass with
soured cream and capers 131
asparagus: asparagus cigarillos 84
asparagus, mozzarella and
peashoots 167
roast asparagus with marcona
almonds 139
tagliatelle with roast
asparagus 111
Turkish chicken stew with sumac
yogurt 130
aubergines: aubergine with toasted
goat's cheese 142
aubergine yogurt 124
avocados: avocado, coriander and
lime dip 78
avocado, Parmesan and salad
sprouts 165
chilli-avo sauce 128
guacamole 101

B

beetroot: beetroot, watermelon and
goat's curd 165
buttered beetroot soup 70
quail egg salad 168
roast beetroot with toasted
crottins 146
blackcurrant cheesecake,
Parisian 175
blinis, rarebit 83
blue cheese, American dip 78
Boursin, touch of 82

Brazil nut pangrattato 110
bread: anchovy toasts with cavolo
nero 53
croutons 74
fennel, Dolcelatte and rosemary
pizza 92
fig, Gorgonzola and basil
croutes 88
French toastie 95
garlic bread 53
metro chilli quesadillas 101
Parma ham and goat's cheese
on toast 94
rarebit blinis 83
walnut and rye soda bread 74
bresaola: labna 46
broccoli: broccoli and coriander
soup 61
broccoli and apple 120
broccoli and quinoa pilaf 107
buckwheat pancakes 187
bulgar wheat: spinach and
anchovy bulgar-otto 115
burgers, halloumi 91
buttermilk 23
buttermilk and chia seed
sauce 121
buttermilk dressing 168
porridge with buttermilk and
cinnamon 184
butternut squash: butternut and
Taleggio pot roast 143
butternut chips with date and
mint quark 149
roast squash, chilli and coriander
soup 67
butter 22–5, 39
classic butters 53
salted butters 54
savoury butters 50, 58, 138
sweet butters 49
whipped butters 49–51
burrata with figs 88

C

cacik 156
cake, chocolate, pear and chilli 172
calcium 14–15
avocado, Parmesan and salad
sprouts 165

carrots: carrot, hazelnut and thyme
soup 62
cumin-roast carrots with
Ossau-Iraty 151
cauliflower: cauliflower soup 64
eggs with smoky cauliflower and
Manchego 152
roast cauliflower cheese 137
saffron cauliflower rice 138
cavolo nero, anchovy toasts with 53
celery, apple and Gorgonzola
soup 62
cheese 26–29
American blue cheese dip 78
cheddar and chutney melt 94
cheese 'n' chilli eats 83
French toastie 95
metro chilli quesadillas 101
rarebit blinis with piccalilli 83
roast cauliflower cheese with
coriander seeds 137
three cheese and tomato
muffins 98
toasted crottins 146
very tomatoey mac 'n' cheese 113
see also individual types of
cheese
cheesecake, Parisian
blackcurrant 175
cherries: pistachio and cherry
slice 176
chicken: chicken and spelt with
buttermilk sauce 121
chicken meatballs 123
chicken tikka masala 127
chicken with za'atar and
aubergine yogurt 124
Mexican smoky chicken and
pepper stew 118
roast chicken with cider
gravy 120
Turkish chicken stew 130
chicken liver and port pâté,
café-style 77
chillies: cheese 'n' chilli eats 83
chilli-avo sauce 128
chocolate, pear and chilli
cake 172
metro chilli quesadillas 101
riccioli with lemon and chilli 114

roast squash, chilli and coriander
soup 67
chips, butternut 149
chocolate: chocolate nut butter 49
chocolate, pear and chilli cake 172
milk chocolate mousse 177
Comté fondue with dippers 97
corn cobs with lime and star anise
butter 138
courgettes: chicken meatballs with
tahini cream 123
grilled courgettes and figs 150
cream 30–3
cream cheese 46
crème brûlée 178
crottins, toasted 146
croutes and croutons 74
halloumi croutons 64
fig, Gorgonzola and basil
croutes 88
cucumber: cacik 156
chilled cucumber, hazelnut and
yogurt soup 63
cucumber raita 68, 133
gazpacho salad 159
curry: chicken tikka masala 127
masala lentil soup 68
prawn and tamarind curry 133

D

dates: butternut chips with date
and mint quark 149
Gorgonzola-stuffed dates 178
dips 75–82
Dolcelatte: fennel, Dolcelatte and
rosemary pizza 92

E

eggs: crème brûlée 178
eggs with smoky cauliflower and
Manchego 152
French toastie 95
quail egg salad 168
Spanish omelette 87

F

fennel, Dolcelatte and rosemary
pizza 92
feta: asparagus cigarillos 84
broccoli and quinoa pilaf with
crispy feta 107

feta yogurt 59
French beans, figs and feta 160
Greek salad stack 159

figs: burrata with figs 88
fig, Gorgonzola and basil croutes 88
French beans, figs and feta 160
grilled courgettes and figs 150

fish: roast seabass with soured cream and capers 131
smoked mackerel and horseradish pâté 75
smoked salmon, lemon and quark pâté 75

fondue, Comté 97
French toastie 95
fritters, pea and Parmesan 140
fromage frais 37, 46
pistachio and cherry slice 176
touch of Boursin 82

G

garlic: garlic bread 53
garlic butter 53
gazpacho salad with Manchego and olives 159
gin and lemon delight 185
ginger: double ginger butter 49
gnocchi, spinach and ricotta 104
goat's cheese: aubergine with toasted goat's cheese 142
beetroot, watermelon and goat's curd 165
goat's cheese appetiser 82
Parma ham and goat's cheese on toast 94
roasted red pepper, goat's cheese and mint dip 81
toasted crottins 146
Gorgonzola: celery, apple and Gorgonzola soup 62
farfalle with roasted tomatoes and Gorgonzola 114
fig, Gorgonzola and basil croutes 88
Gorgonzola-stuffed dates 178
granola, frozen yogurt sundae 182
Greek salad stack 159
green goddess ricotta 81

guacamole 101
guinea fowl with chilli-avo sauce 128

H

halloumi: halloumi croutons 64
grilled halloumi with cos and almond salad 161
halloumi burgers with lemon and mint 91
halloumi-harissa roast veg 149
hazelnuts: carrot, hazelnut and thyme soup 62
chilled cucumber, hazelnut and yogurt soup 63
spelt and hazelnut-stuffed mushrooms 108
herbs: herb bread 53
herb butter 53
pesto 110
horseradish: smoked mackerel and horseradish pâté 75

I

ice cream: honey yogurt ice cream 184
raspberry yogurt ice cream 182

L

labna 46
lactose intolerance 38–9
recipes 53, 62, 64, 74, 78, 83, 88, 91, 92, 94, 101, 108, 111, 113, 114, 115, 133, 137, 138, 139, 143, 145, 149, 151, 162, 165, 166, 167, 172, 178
lemons: gin and lemon delight 185
salad of Romaine, pear and Parmesan 160
lentils: masala lentil soup 68

M

Manchego: eggs with smoky cauliflower and Manchego 152
gazpacho salad with Manchego 159
masala lentil soup 68
meatballs, chicken 123
metro chilli quesadillas 101
Mexican smoky chicken and pepper stew 118

milk 18–21
mimolette: salad of mimolette and crushed walnuts 162
minerals 14–15
miso butter 50, 58
mousse, milk chocolate 177
mozzarella: asparagus, mozzarella and peashoots 167
Parma ham, olive and mozzarella cocktail 166
muffins, three cheese and tomato 98
mushrooms: mushroom soup 69
spelt and hazelnut-stuffed mushrooms 108

N

nut butter, chocolate 49

O

oatmeal: porridge with buttermilk and cinnamon 184
olives: gazpacho salad with Manchego and olives 159
Greek salad stack 159
Parma ham, olive and mozzarella cocktail 166
omelette, Spanish 87
Ossau-Iraty, cumin-roast carrots with 151

P

pancakes, buckwheat 187
pangrattato, Brazil nut 110
panna cotta, vanilla 181
Parisian blackcurrant cheesecake 175
Parma ham: asparagus cigarillos 84
metro chilli quesadillas 101
Parma ham and goat's cheese on toast 94
Parma ham, olive and mozzarella cocktail 166
roast seabass with soured cream and capers 131
Parmesan: avocado, Parmesan and salad sprouts 165
pea and Parmesan fritters 140
salad of Romaine, pear and Parmesan 160

pasta: farfalle with roasted tomatoes and Gorgonzola 114
linguine with pesto and Brazil nut pangrattato 110
riccioli with lemon and chilli 114
tagliatelle with roast asparagus 111
very tomatoey mac 'n' cheese 113
pâtés 75–7
pea and Parmesan fritters 140
pears: chocolate, pear and chilli cake 172
salad of Romaine, pear and Parmesan 160
peashoots, asparagus, mozzarella and 167
peppers: Abondance and almond pepper rarebits 145
Mexican smoky chicken and pepper stew 118
party peppadews 83
Piment d'Espelette and lemon butter 50
roasted red pepper, goat's cheese and mint dip 81
pesto: mushroom soup with spelt, pesto and yogurt 69
rocket pesto 142
pilaf: broccoli and quinoa pilaf 107
spicy spelt pilaf 105
pistachios: pistachio and cherry slice 176
watercress and pistachio soup 58
pizza, fennel, Dolcelatte and rosemary 92
porridge with buttermilk 184
pot roast, butternut and Taleggio 143
potatoes: Spanish omelette 87
prawn and tamarind curry 133

Q

quail egg salad 168
quark 46
butternut chips with date and mint quark 149
gin and lemon delight 185
milk chocolate mousse 177

index

Parisian blackcurrant
cheesecake 175
smoked salmon, lemon and
quark pâté 75
quesadillas, metro chilli 101
quinoa and broccoli pilaf 107

R
raisins: apple and goji berry
yogurt 45
raita, cucumber 68, 133
rarebit: Abondance and almond
pepper rarebits 145
rarebit blinis with piccalilli 83
raspberry yogurt 45
raspberry yogurt ice cream 182
rice, five-hour orange 181
ricotta: chilli-avo sauce 128
green goddess ricotta 81
spinach and ricotta gnocchi 104
rocket pesto 142
Roquefort: American blue cheese
dip 78

S
saffron: saffron cauliflower rice 138
saffron yogurt 105
salads: asparagus, mozzarella and
peashoots 167
beetroot, watermelon and goat's
curd 165
cacik 156
avocado, Parmesan and salad
sprouts 165
French beans, figs and feta 160

gazpacho salad with Manchego
and olives 159
Greek salad stack 159
grilled halloumi with cos and
almond salad 161
Parma ham, olive and mozzarella
cocktail 166
quail egg salad 168
salad of mimolette and crushed
walnuts 162
salad of Romaine, pear and
Parmesan 160
soups: broccoli and coriander 61
buttered beetroot 70
carrot, hazelnut and thyme 62
cauliflower 64
chilled cucumber, hazelnut and
yogurt 63
masala lentil 68
mushroom 69
roast squash, chilli and
coriander 67
sweet potato and cumin 59
watercress and pistachio 58
soured cream 30
recipes using 67, 75, 77, 78, 87,
105, 118, 121, 127, 130, 131
Spanish omelette 87
spelt: chicken and spelt with
buttermilk sauce 121
mushroom soup with spelt, pesto
and yogurt 69
spelt and hazelnut-stuffed
mushrooms 108
spicy spelt pilaf 105

spinach: spinach and anchovy
bulgar-otto 115
spinach and ricotta gnocchi 104
stews: Mexican smoky chicken and
pepper stew 118
Turkish chicken stew 130
strawberry yogurt 45
sumac yogurt 130
sweet potato and cumin soup 59

T
tahini cream 61, 123
Taleggio and butternut pot roast 143
tikka masala, chicken 127
toastie, French 95
tomatoes: farfalle with roasted
tomatoes and Gorgonzola 114
gazpacho salad 159
Greek salad stack 159
three cheese and tomato
muffins 98
tomato and rose petal butter 50
very tomatoey mac 'n' cheese 113
tortillas: metro chilli quesadillas 101
Turkish chicken stew 130

V
vanilla: vanilla cinnamon butter 49
vanilla panna cotta 181
vanilla yogurt 45
vegetables: guinea fowl with chilli-
avo sauce 128
halloumi-harissa roast veg 149
vitamins 15–16

W
walnuts: salad of mimolette and
crushed walnuts 162
walnut and rye soda bread 74
watercress: labna 46
watercress and pistachio soup 58
watermelon: beetroot, watermelon
and goat's curd 165

Y
yogurt 34–7, 42, 43
aubergine yogurt 124
cacik 156
chilled cucumber, hazelnut and
yogurt soup 63
chunky cucumber raita 133
feta yogurt 59
flavoured yogurts 45
frozen granola yogurt
sundae 182
Greek yogurt 34, 43
grilled courgettes and figs with a
yogurt dressing 150
honey yogurt ice cream 184
mushroom soup with spelt,
pesto and yogurt 69
raspberry yogurt ice cream 182
saffron yogurt 105
sumac yogurt 130
vanilla panna cotta 181

Z
za'atar: chicken with za'atar and
aubergine yogurt 124
za'atar butter 50

acknowledgements

A big thank you to Kyle Cathie for sowing the seed for a book on dairy, that proved such a fascinating foray into the nutritional science of this extraordinary foodstuff; also to Claire Rogers, for co-ordinating the project and being a pleasure to work with.

Thank you to my 'dream team' – the photographer Con Poulos and his assistant Garth McKee for the stunning photography, and Susie Theodorou and her team of cooks, for your magical touch and styling of the recipes. For the beautiful, calm and minimal design, thanks to Erika Oliveira and her production assistant Hollis Yungbliut; and to Stephanie Evans for the careful copy editing.

It was a huge pleasure to work with the nutritionist Alina Tierney, who kept the science on track and methodically addressed every detail. I am also very grateful to Juliet Harbutt, creator of the British Cheese Awards, for sharing her expertise. Many thanks to Angela Mason, Associate Editor of *You Magazine* in the *Mail on Sunday*, for all her support

And finally, to Jonnie, Louis and Rothko, who are the inspiration for everything I cook, and whose judgement I trust implicitly, as I do my agent Lizzy Kremer at David Higham. Thank you for being there.